Norman T. Carrington MA

Brodie's Notes on Thomas Hardy's

The Mayor of Casterbridge

Pan Educational London and Sydney

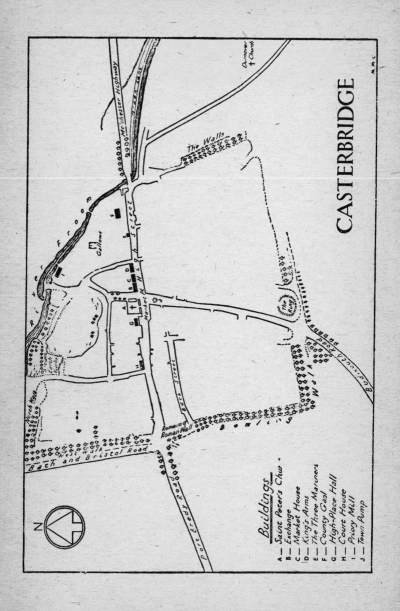

CASTERBRIDGE

N

Buildings

A — Saint Peter's Church
B — Exchange
C — Market House
D — King's Arms
E — The Three Mariners
F — County Gaol
G — High-Place Hall
H — Court House
I — Priory Mill
J — Town Pump

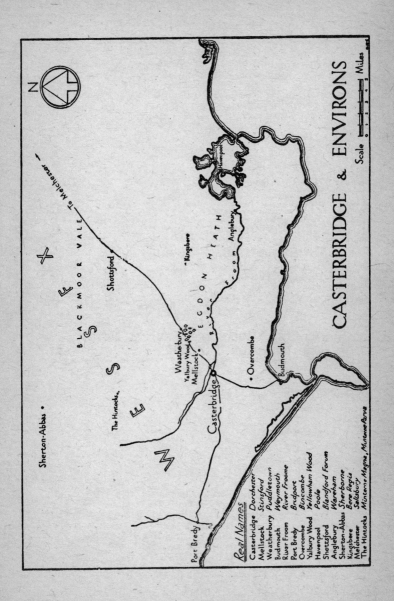

N

CASTERBRIDGE & ENVIRONS

Scale [====] Miles
0 1 2 3 4 5

to Melchester

BLACKMOOR VALE

Sherton-Abbas •

The Hintocks •

Shottsford

Weatherbury
Yalbury Wood
Mellstock

"Kingsbere

EGDON HEATH

River Froom

Anglebury

Casterbridge

• Overcombe

Budmouth

Port Bredy

Liverpool

Real Names

Casterbridge	Dorchester
Mellstock	Stinsford
Weatherbury	Puddletown
Budmouth	Weymouth
River Froom	River Froome
Port Bredy	Bridport
Overcombe	Boscombe
Yalbury Wood	Yellowham Wood
Havenpool	Poole
Shottsford	Blandford Forum
Anglebury	Wareham
Sherton-Abbas	Sherborne
Kingsbere	Bere Regis
Melchester	Salisbury
The Hintocks	Minterne Magna, Minterne Parva

3

CONTENTS

First published by James Brodie Ltd
This edition published 1976 by Pan Books Ltd,
Cavaye Place, London SW10 9PG
4 5 6 7 8 9
© James Brodie Ltd 1964
ISBN 0 330 50012 0
Printed and bound in Great Britain by
Richard Clay (The Chaucer Press) Ltd, Bungay, Suffolk

This book is sold subject to the condition that it
shall not, by way of trade or otherwise, be lent, re-sold,
hired out or otherwise circulated without the publisher's prior
consent in any form of binding or cover other than that in which
it is published and without a similar condition including this
condition being imposed on the subsequent purchaser

THE MAYOR OF CASTERBRIDGE

THE AUTHOR

Thomas Hardy was born on 2nd June, 1840, the eldest child of a master mason (we should call him a builder) of the village of Upper Bockhampton, in the parish of Stinsford, near Dorchester. His father was comfortably off and well content with his lot, not caring to follow his wife's advice and move into a bigger place offering more custom. His business was a good one for a village. He employed no fewer than fifteen men at one time, including his neighbour the tranter, who carted all his building materials. Things in the village were much as Hardy describes them in *Under the Greenwood Tree*. This secluded and self-contained community was, as yet, unaffected by the machine age (though the railway came to Dorchester when Hardy was seven years old).

As a child Hardy was very forward but not over strong, and he was eight before he started school. First he went to the village school at Lower Bockhampton (Fancy Day's school) and a year later to a private school in Dorchester. He worked hard and became a good " all-rounder " in his studies, showing particular aptitude for Latin. He was a shy boy, very much in earnest. In his leisure time his father taught him to play the violin and prepare manuscript music for himself. One of his first presents from his father was a toy accordion. His father was a fiddler in the west gallery of Stinsford Church choir, one much in demand at country festivals. Hardy's father, grandfather and great-grandfather had all been in the choir and master masons in Stinsford. It was a coveted hereditary honour in the family to play in the choir. After school and in the holidays father often took the boy with him when he was playing at weddings and parties in the neighbourhood. His mother was an omnivorous reader, fond of good books, and she took care to see that her son had plenty, though not the kind one would provide for a child to-day, for example, Dryden's *Virgil* and Dr. Johnson's *Rasselas*. She had taught him to read by the time he was three. She was a good singer too, and he loved the old ballads that she used to sing to him. The tune *Miss M'Leod of Ayr* (XVI) he learnt from her.

While the boy was wondering if his skill in Latin would lead to a career in the Church, in 1856 his father arranged for him to become a pupil of John Hicks, a Dorchester ecclesiastical architect, whom he had met in business when working to his designs. Young Thomas pursued his studies when working hours were over, and taught himself Greek as well as improving his Latin. Speaking of his life as a young man of twenty, Hardy wrote that " the professional life, the scholar's life, and the rustic life combined in the twenty-four hours of the day." To this period belong a few poems, but they were not published. His work as an architect's pupil was always his first concern, however : Thomas Hardy never undertook anything to which he could not give of his best.

Thus in 1862 he went to London as " a young Gothic draughtsman who could restore and design churches and rectory houses ", in the offices of A. W. Blomfield, a leading London architect. Straightway in the same year he won the R.I.B.A. Essay prize, and the success of his entry was in no small measure due to its literary quality. He followed this up by winning the Institute's prize and medal the following year. Some eight years later, together with another architect, he had his designs for schools accepted in a competition arranged by the London School Board. His first published work was in *Chambers's Journal* in March, 1865—*How I Built Myself a House*, a gently ironical piece, easily written. The student will remember the many architectural terms in *The Mayor of Casterbridge*.

All this time he was getting more and more interested in literature—not only in the great classics of our race, but in the exciting contemporary publications of the eighteen-sixties. He thought seriously on what he read—Thomas Hardy accepted nothing lightly. He had developed an interest in art too, and at one time had a firm intention of becoming an art critic. There are many references to art in *The Mayor of Casterbridge, e.g.* to Correggio (XVI), Titian (XXII) or the Tuscan school (XXVI).

In 1867 he returned to Dorchester as an assistant to his old principal, Mr. Hicks. In *The Mayor of Casterbridge* he dwells caressingly on all the features of the town. It was now, back at home, that he started to write fiction. His first effort was not accepted, and the second, *Desperate Remedies,* rejected by Macmillan (later to be his publishers), was accepted only at his own risk by a lesser-known house (1871). He lost on it financially, remainder copies of the novel were, in fact, sold off cheaply, but he had the satisfaction of seeing a novel in print.

Setbacks can be more significant than successes, however, and the young novelist had realised where his skill lay—not in sensational incident but in description of the Dorset countryside and people, and he set about writing *Under the Greenwood Tree*. Thus early in 1871 he was back at Bockhampton once more, among the scenes of his boyhood. In 1872 the novel was accepted by Tinsley Bros. at their risk, in fact they paid £30 for the copyright ! Hardy did not feel confident enough in 1872 to publish under his own name, and no wonder, for the *Spectator* reviewer of *Desperate Remedies* welcomed an anonymity that would save disgrace to the family name. Further, if he let his employers know that he spent his time writing novels, and unsuccessful ones at that, it might affect his business reputation. He need not have feared. *Under the Greenwood Tree*, if not an immediate success, was no failure, here, or in America the next year.

But the secret had leaked out in the publishing world. One day Hardy received a letter from the new editor of the *Cornhill Magazine*, saying that he had much admired the freshness of *Under the Greenwood Tree*, and enquiring if he would write a serial for the *Cornhill*. He was too busy at the moment writing *A Pair of Blue Eyes* for *Tinsley's Magazine*, but promised his next work. The result was his first great novel, *Far from the Madding Crowd*, in the *Cornhill* for the whole of 1874. It was an immediate success, and was published no fewer than seven times in its first year, in the *Cornhill* (anonymously), as a complete volume separately in England and U.S.A. (in November), and in four American magazines. It turned out to be Hardy's best seller after *Tess of the D'Urbervilles*. He now felt quite safe in giving up work as an architect for good, and on his royalties from the book he married a Cornish woman of his own age whom he had met over four years before while doing architectural work on a church Hicks had been instructed to restore. It was she who, in 1871, when he was disappointed, encouraged him to stick to literature. Hardy's retiring nature is shown in his quiet wedding. Only two witnesses were present—nobody from Hardy's family. At first the couple were happy, but their opposite disposition and characters eventually brought them to lead separate lives.

—I am here, and you are there,
And a hundred miles between !

Hardy and his wife were not close in feeling, and the lack of inspiration in their marriage from day to day may have been one reason for the growing gloom and pessimism of his later novels.

After *Far from the Madding Crowd* Hardy went from success to success (though not all his novels met with popular approval)—*The Return of the Native* (1878), *The Trumpet-Major* (1880), *The Mayor of Casterbridge* (1886), first as a serial in *The Graphic* (see p. 21), *The Woodlanders* (1887), *Tess of the D'Urbervilles* (1891), *Jude the Obscure* (1894).

The last, so out of keeping with Victorian sentiment, was attacked so fiercely that Hardy decided once and for all, " No more novel-writing for me ! " just as Henchard might have done—" I'll never trouble 'ee again, Elizabeth-Jane— no, not to my dying day ! Good-night. Good-bye ! " Instead, at his home at Max Gate, Dorchester, he returned to poetry. (Max Gate was designed by himself, and he lived there from 1883 until his death.) It is seldom that a poet writes his best poetry after he is fifty, as Hardy did. It is a pity that some poets (Wordsworth, for instance) did not *stop* writing poetry when they were fifty.

In 1912 his wife died. In 1914 he married Miss Florence Dugdale, an author of children's stories, an Enfield woman of Dorset stock, who had often helped him with his writing when his eyes were bad, and had looked up material for him in the Library of the British Museum. There was nearly forty years' disparity in age between them, but it is a pleasure to record that her love, devotion and admiration, and her unceasing care for his welfare, made his last years supremely happy. Later she became one of his first biographers. He lived a quiet life—he described himself as aloof rather than shy. His pleasures were simple, and not until he became too feeble to cycle would he buy a car. He was acknowledged to be the greatest living English novelist, a position he had reached with no regular school and University education, but now three Universities were happy to honour him (and themselves) by awarding him the honorary degree of D.Litt. His works continued to be in great demand and he left a fortune of nearly £100,000. He tried to keep off would-be admirers, could never be persuaded to talk about himself, and shrank from making speeches—the very reverse of his contemporary George Bernard Shaw, the pushing publicity man. The honour he appreciated most was the Freedom of Dorchester—more even than the Order of Merit with which he was invested in the same year (1910). His last public appearance was in 1927, when he laid the foundation stone of the new buildings of Dorchester Grammar School, of which he had been a Governor for many years. His love of music continued to the end, and his violin and 'cello always stood in a corner by the bookcase in his study.

He lived to see wagons disappear before the motor-lorry and the villagers' isolation further broken down by radio in cottage homes. He died on 11th January, 1928. His ashes were laid in Poets' Corner, Westminster Abbey, with a spadeful of Dorset earth thrown over them, but his heart was buried in Stinsford Churchyard, a very happy symbolical compromise.

Page references in these Notes are to the edition in Macmillan's " Scholar's Library ", but chapter numbers are always given and the notes can be used with any edition of the text.

THE BOOK

Plot

The story arises from a hay-trusser's love of drink, and his
energy and hard work. In drunken irritability Michael
Henchard sells his wife (and little girl) to a sailor at a fair
one night. Returning to his senses next morning he takes
a solemn vow not to touch strong drink for twenty-one
years (the age he is now). All efforts to find his wife fail.

By his energy and hard work he builds up a good corn and
hay business and in time becomes Mayor of Casterbridge.
Exactly eighteen years afterwards his wife returns with her
daughter (supposing her sailor " husband " to be dead).
Henchard and she keep their relationship secret, and he
courts her and marries her again. Henchard's business
grows bigger under the capable management of a young
Scot, Donald Farfrae, but Henchard quarrels with Farfrae,
who sets up on his own and soon becomes a formidable
rival. Mrs. Henchard dies. Henchard finds out that her
daughter, whom he thought to be his (and, indeed, whom he
had told that she was) is the sailor's daughter.

Farfrae rises as Henchard falls. He marries the woman
Henchard expects to marry. He buys his business when he
goes bankrupt and lives in his house. Henchard's degradation is complete when his past becomes known and he takes
to drink once more (the twenty-one years being gone).

His step-daughter, whom he had at first treated roughly
when he discovered that she was not his, in due time wins
her way to his heart and turns out to be his only comfort in
life, but she is now claimed by the sailor, who comes to
Casterbridge to find her, and she is disgusted by the deceit
of Henchard, who had concealed her parentage from her.
Finally, she marries Farfrae, whose wife has died, and
Henchard turns his back on the town, and comes to a
wretched end in a tumbledown cottage.

Structure

The Mayor of Casterbridge is a one-man story, as the sub-
title said, " A Story of a Man of Character " (*i.e.* strong
character, not necessarily good or bad). The Mayor
dominates the story from his appearance as a hay-trusser
" of fine figure ", to the peak of his fortune as the chief

citizen of Casterbridge, until the wheel comes full circle and
he goes out of the town a hay-trusser—as he came into
Weydon-Priors at the start. The climax of his social status
is just before the trial of the furmity-woman. Hardy says
so himself. " Small as the police-court incident had been in
itself, it formed the edge or turn in the incline of Henchard's
fortunes. On that day—almost at that minute—he passed
the ridge of prosperity and honour, and began to descend
rapidly on the other side." Elsewhere Hardy calls the
Mayoral banquet his " Austerlitz " ; he continued to do
well in business after the days of the " growed-wheat ",
but it must be admitted that Farfrae was the agent.
Henchard's material downfall in business begins with
Farfrae's over-riding his decision in the hay-yard.

> ' Hullo, hullo ! ' said Henchard, coming up behind. ' Who's
> sending him back ? '
> All the men looked towards Farfrae.
> ' I am, ' said Donald. ' I say this joke has been carried far
> enough. '
> ' And I say it hasn't ! Get up in the waggon, Whittle. '
> ' Not if I am manager, ' said Farfrae. ' He either goes home, or
> I march out of this yard for good. '

His spiritual downfall begins with his wife's death and his
discovery that Elizabeth-Jane is not his daughter.

The opening of the story is characteristic of Hardy. A
man and a woman come into view on a road approaching a
village. They are described. Then one of them speaks and
the action begins.

The first two chapters are a prologue giving the background to the story proper, which opens with the coming of
Mrs. Henchard and her daughter to look for their " relative "
(III), who, to their surprise turns out to be the Mayor of
the town.

Qualities of character that have made Henchard mayor
cause his downfall—energy, determination and impulsive
action. The purpose of Farfrae and Elizabeth-Jane in the
structure of the novel is for character-contrast with
Henchard. In the end they marry, as we knew they must do
in the beginning, their fortunes in the meantime providing
part of the suspense that holds the reader. Notice how
Farfrae dogs the steps of Henchard through the book. He
comes into possession of his business, his house, his civic

position, the woman whom Henchard regarded as his wife by rights, and finally his stepdaughter. Both Farfrae's marriages rob Henchard of what he holds dearest at the time.

There is thus a sense of balance and pattern in the structure of the book. Similarly when Henchard and Susan remarry each has a hidden secret : her secret is the identity of Elizabeth-Jane, his is Lucetta. (And they both have a secret from Elizabeth-Jane.)

The contrasts between characters important in the structure of the story are dealt with separately in their appropriate section. Notice too the contrasts between tragedy and comedy, throwing one another up, for example, the racy, worldly-wise humorous talk of the rustics after Mrs. Henchard's death ; and the dead goldfinch, and what it signifies, amidst the happiness of Elizabeth-Jane's first few days of married life.

The story is told with economy. Events important in the plot are told in detail ; others of less significance are passed over quickly—with one exception, the rescue by Henchard of Lucetta and Elizabeth-Jane from the bull (XXIX).

In Hardy's novels there are many coincidences, indeed, he realised it himself (see p. 21). The reader must decide for himself whether he considers such past the realm of probability, that is, whether they leave him with the impression that they are dictated by the structure of the story instead of arising naturally from it. Newson's return to life is very hard to credit.

Notice in this connection the number of overheard conversations.

1. The conversation of the two lovers in the market-place, overheard by Farfrae and Lucetta, which unites their hearts in a common bond of sympathy (for lovers), thus increasing their own regard for one another (XXIII).

2. Where Henchard, behind a wheat-shock, hears Farfrae and Lucetta making love to one another in the cornfields (XXVII).

3. The conversation between Henchard and Farfrae, overheard by Lucetta, as Henchard reads out passages from her letters (XXXV).

4. Where Henchard, hiding behind a wall, hears Farfrae address his stepdaughter as " Dearest Elizabeth-Jane " and then kiss her (XLII).

It must be remembered, however, that 2, 3 and 4 were not accidental : they were the result of character ; in each case the person who overhears the conversation is *deliberately* eavesdropping. There are other less important instances, *e.g.* where Elizabeth-Jane hears Farfrae suggest to Henchard that they should not go about together so much, a hint of their coming differences, or where Henchard's jealousy is increased by his overhearing Farfrae's praises (XVI).

Other coincidences are the sudden turn of the wind which ruins Henchard, the return of the furmity-woman and Newson's coming to life again just at the right time (the wrong time for Henchard). Indeed, Newson stops in Casterbridge only until three days after the wedding, when his joy in his daughter's welfare evaporates, and he can be got out of the way once more. Again, however, the bad effect on Henchard of the first of these coincidences is due to his character as much as the vagaries of the weather. Had Henchard not been so superstitious and trusted an old soothsayer, and had he not through his bitter hatred sought to get an underhand advantage over Farfrae, he would not have bought grain so heavily.

But the one coincidence that no attempt is made to explain and of which no mention is made in the story, is that Henchard should have forgotten the date of his daughter's birthday, or, alternatively, that both Elizabeth-Janes were born on the same day of the year.

Theme

The theme of a novel reveals the author's reading of the life he portrays. *The Mayor of Casterbridge* shows that no satisfaction can be founded on deceit. Its motto might be " Truth will out ", or " Be sure your sins will find you out ". Henchard would have been a happier man if he could have looked everyone in the face without fearful secrets gnawing at his heart's content. He piles up evil on evil, which for shame has to be hid, from the wife-selling episode in the first chapter to the despicable lie to Elizabeth-Jane's father that she is dead. "Above all things, tell no untruth, no

not in trifles, " wrote Sir Philip Sidney's father to him when
he was a boy at school. " And let it not satisfy you that,
for a time, the hearers take it for truth, for afterwards, it
will be known for what it is, to your shame. " So Henchard's
lies are to no purpose. " The secret would be yours and mine
only ", Henchard had fondly said to his wife when planning
their re-marriage, but all the lies of his life are revealed one
by one for what they are. The chief character of the book,
at one time a most successful character in terms of worldly
fortune, is in reality a failure.

Lucetta's deceit similarly gives her a haunting worry
beneath the superficial happiness of her marriage. " I
won't be a slave to the past ", she had impetuously cried
(XXV, 203), but it was the past that killed her. " Ah ",
says Farfrae afterwards, " I doubt there will be any good
in secrets ! A secret cast a deep shadow over my life "
(XLII, 349).

Beyond this, at the heart of the novel there is a sense of
the cruel irony of life. Not one character in the book has a
happy life, not one radiates happiness and charm. There is
no sunny laughter. Hardy sums up his philosophy (as
Elizabeth-Jane's) in the last paragraph. It is the key-note
of *The Mayor of Casterbridge*. Life gives bitter blows. So
it comes about that Henchard discovers that Elizabeth-
Jane is not his own on the very night he has told her that
she is, when thinking it over, she believes that she must be
and agrees to call him " father " ; that he asks her to change
her mind and go on living with him just " ten minutes too
late. She was in the fly—was already, in imagination, at
the house of the lady whose manner had such charms for
her " ; that Farfrae wins Lucetta's heart three minutes
before Henchard pays her a visit, a visit he has purposely
delayed through his own wounded pride ; that the furmity-
woman and Newson come back just when they do. " That
it should have happened then ! " we hear people say. The
sense of an inscrutable fate overlooking man's life hangs
over *The Mayor of Casterbridge*, and it is this feeling in
Hardy's novels that makes people call them " pessimistic ".
" Henchard, like all his kind, was superstitious, and he
could not help thinking that the concatenation of events
this evening had produced was the scheme of some sinister
intelligence bent on punishing him." Elizabeth-Jane felt

it too. " Everybody and everything seem against you so ",
she divined. She feels it for herself. Even the best in life,
Hardy would say, leaves little to be thankful for. The attitude to life of that " single-hearted girl ", the best character
in the book, is that she must take what comes and bear up
against it. *The Mayor of Casterbridge* is a novel of dis-
illusionment, of helplessness in the face of the circumstances
of life. H. C. Duffin* goes so far as to call it " the most
hopeless book ever written. The tone of the telling, in the
latter half of the story, is stony despair ". There is certainly
more pain than pleasure in *The Mayor of Casterbridge*. Hardy
would, of course, say that this is life.

The novel ends with the joys of the marriage of the girl
who fell in love early in the book and whose fortunes we
have been following since she turned away from the window
and reflected, " I was nothing to him, and there was no
reason why he should have wished me good-bye." But it
ends in a minor key none the less.

Preponderance of trouble and unhappiness, however,
does not in itself make a book pessimistic. It depends on
man's reaction to it. Some men can redeem misfortune and
make it glorious by the way they face it, and thus its final
effect is not pessimistic. The only way those in *The Mayor
of Casterbridge* meet the mischances of life is to endure them
defiantly, or, at best, bravely. They do not come out of their
experience finer than they went in.

Background

The town of Casterbridge is the Dorchester near where
Hardy was brought up, where he obtained his first job on
leaving school and where he lived nearly all his life. Hardy
had an abiding affection for the town and the surrounding
Dorset countryside. His pictures of it are true and clear and
vivid, and beautifully described with the touch of an artist.

The best way to see the importance of the background
is to call to mind some incident in the book, and it is
certain that the place where it happened will be associated
with the recollection and the feeling about it. Like Scott,
Hardy found great inspiration in the sights and manners
and customs of his own neighbourhood. If he looked at a
scene he could imagine the events taking place there before

Thomas Hardy.

his eyes, as if the town buildings and the market-place were waiting to be peopled. The way that Hardy has the actual locality in mind is shown clearly by comparing his towns and villages with the real places. Incidentally, the very names he chooses give a local colour of their own. In this thin disguising of names he is followed by J. B. Priestley in our own time. It is merely mechanical, of course, but what is important is that it shows his strong sense of locality.

Hardy is particularly sensitive to the beauties of the town in the evening and early morning. Casterbridge is first described as Elizabeth-Jane and her mother walk in from Weydon-Priors at nightfall, next as Elizabeth goes up the High Street in the early morning. Weydon-Priors, a smaller version of the big market-town, was similarly first described at nightfall, and again in the bright stillness of the next morning.

The business of the market was done in the streets, as usual in those days. " The farmers as a rule preferred the open *carrefour* for their transactions, despite its inconvenient jostlings and the danger from crossing vehicles, to the gloomy sheltered market-room provided for them " (XXII, 175). Market-day in Dorchester is still on a Saturday. The litter left in the streets after the market was seed and straw that the sparrows were feeding on, not the dirty bits of paper that deface the street to-day.

Some buildings are of stone (*e.g.* High-Place Hall), many of the houses are timbered, and the disreputable quarters of Mixen Lane consist of thatched cottages with sanded floors (XLI, 336). Many of Hardy's buildings can still be seen in the modern Dorchester.

The goods sold in the shops of Casterbridge are those of which a farming community stands in need, a feature which the visitor stills notices in Dorchester (IV. 31–32). The shops are open as long as there is a chance of customers. So are the inns. It is a convivial custom for choir and churchgoers to go over to the inn after Sunday afternoon service. Church music in those days was made by a choir of instrumentalists, not by an organ. (*Under the Greenwood Tree* sees the replacement of the one by the other.) A drop of smuggled liquor can be obtained on the cheap by those in the know.

Life goes on at a much slower pace than to-day. People seldom seem short of time to stop and have a chat—very different from the impatient *tempo* of modern life. Their lives have a leisurely air, and yet men had to work long hours, in an age when a labourer worked as long as he was told. In the normal way farm-labourers worked a ten-hour day, not including meal breaks : they went out early in the morning and returned home for breakfast : Farfrae himself sets out before six in the morning (XXXIV) : a waggoner starts work at six, and if his employer tells him to be there at four, he is at his employer's mercy, and as likely as not to be without a job at all unless he complies. For this he earned eight shillings per week (overtime payments were a matter of grace) : a maid earned £12 a year : and sixpence was a good present. The labouring classes, like Abel Whittle, were unable to read and write. Some of the employers even, were poor hands with a pen (XX, 149).

In those days ordinary folk walked to where they wanted to go. When the book opens Henchard and Susan have been walking all day, and eighteen years later when Elizabeth-Jane and her mother find that they have to go to Casterbridge, it never enters their heads to go any other way than on foot. Heavy loads were taken by wagon, rich men had gigs, and those who could afford it went by public coach. The King's Arms was a coach connecting station. Most people never travelled farther than they could walk in their lives, and the interests of their lives ended at town affairs—town gossip, to put it less kindly.

Life is happy-go-lucky, but more exact methods are coming, even into Casterbridge. " This accomplished young man does it all by ciphering and mensuration." People are getting more conscious of hygiene, but Farfrae's skill is praised only because it " purifies " the dirty wheat, not because it removes the need for purification. " Then the wheat—that sometimes used to taste so strongly of mice when made into bread that people could fairly tell the breed—Farfrae has a plan for purifying, so that nobody would dream the smallest four-legged beast had walked over it once " (XVI, 122). It is left to a stranger from the north, one of a new generation, and above the average townsman in intelligence and education, to introduce a new horse-drill to Casterbridge. This part of the country is slow to accept new ideas. According to Lucetta the town is fifty years behind the times (XXV, 201).

The stocks and the bull stake, surviving as reminders of man's cruelty to man and beast, have now been given up as barbarities of the past, but in their place the common people eagerly anticipate " skimmity-rides " (although such libel-lous exhibitions are frowned on by authority), and toad-bags are much in demand.

Casterbridge is " a place deposited in the block upon a corn-field. There was no suburb in the modern sense, or transitional inter-mixture of town and down ". It is separ-ated from the surrounding farmland by " dark dense old avenues " of trees along its boundaries, but its economic life is bound up with the prosperity of the surrounding country-side, it is the " nerve-knot of the surrounding country life " (IX, 70), " the bell-board on which all the adjacent hamlets and villages sounded their notes " (XXVI, 211).

But this " rare old market-town ", as Hardy affection-ately calls it, is dear to him for what it has been as well as for what it is. " Casterbridge announced old Rome in every street, alley, and precinct." Hardy's style swells with a sense of reverence in the magnificent description of the Ring (XI), " one of the finest Roman Amphitheatres, if not the very finest, remaining in Britain ", he proudly says. " Earthworks square, and not square, were as common as blackberries hereabout " (XVI, 118). He likes the trees of the town walks better because they are planted on the ancient defences ; the weir-pool of Ten Hatches is dearer to him because it is " formed by the wash of centuries ". The visitor to-day cannot help but feel the spell of the past as he treads the streets of Dorchester.

All at once Casterbridge gives way to fields of rich corn-land, woods and open heath cut by dusty roads. But it is not the end of antiquities : not far away are to be found the remains of a fortress of the ancient Britons. And so Caster-bridge and its neighbourhood bear the imprint of the years from prehistoric times, through Roman, to the medieval St. Peter's Church and the friary, to Donald Farfrae, two-hundredth-odd Mayor of the town.

One thing has been the same through all these ages—the weather. The study of literature is a corrective to the fallacy that English weather is getting worse. It could no more be relied on in Hardy's (or Henchard's) day than it can in ours, and sunshine, drizzle and torrential rain occur in about the same proportions in *The Mayor of Casterbridge* as in the real conditions of everyday life.

Sympathetic Background

Sympathetic background is an old device, harmonising the weather with the events in the story, at once intensifying the atmosphere and broadening it, as if not only the two or three people in the story were affected, but the whole universe. It is made use of in the greatest literature and in the cheapest films.

A hay-trusser and his wife are introduced plodding along at the end of a long day's dusty walk, in an attitude of " stale familiarity ". The vegetation tones with the two in the story. It " had entered the blackened-green stage of colour that the doomed leaves pass through on their way to dingy, and yellow, and red ". The dust on the road deadened their footfalls, even as their speech was still. The birds were silent, save for " the voice of a weak bird singing a trite old evening song that might doubtless have been heard on the hill at the same hour, and with the self-same trills, quavers, and breves, at any sunset of that season for centuries untold ". (In passing, notice how even a bird's song links Hardy with the past.) Next morning the man is a different man, and the morning is fresh, sunny and bracing.

As Elizabeth-Jane paces up Casterbridge High Street on a " mellow " morning, about an errand that is to end so fortunately, she can see " through the long, straight, entrance passages " " as through tunnels, the mossy gardens at the back, glowing with nasturtiums, fuchsias, scarlet geraniums, ' bloody warriors ', snapdragons, and dahlias, this floral blaze being backed by crusted grey stone-work remaining from a yet remoter Casterbridge than the venerable one visible in the street ". (The background to the flowers, like the bird's song, returns Hardy to the past.)

In contrast with this colourful scene notice the description of the " melancholy, impressive, lonely " Amphitheatre (XI), where, in spite of its seclusion, meetings of happy lovers seldom had place. " Perhaps it was because its associations had about them something sinister." So its " dismal privacy " was " the frequent spot for appointments of a furtive kind ". Here Henchard met his two women—at dusk (although the second meeting was not at his request). As the plaintive Lucetta neared the amphitheatre, "The sun was resting on the hill like a drop of blood on an eyelid." Farfrae's meetings with Lucetta and with Elizabeth-Jane are in kindlier places. At the beginning of the chapter following Susan's meeting with Henchard, emphasising the gloom by contrast, is a description of Henchard's fragrant garden.

On the morning when a door opens to release Elizabeth-Jane from Henchard's bullying, it is " fairly fine ". On the day she arranges to leave for High-Place Hall " a drizzling rain fell ", but " Elizabeth-Jane, having now changed her orbit from one of gay independence to laborious self-help, thought the weather good enough for such declined glory as hers ". Henchard goes to the " prophet's cot " " one evening when it was raining so heavily that ivy and laurel resounded like distant musketry ", just such weather as that in which Fancy Day went to see Elizabeth Endorfield in *Under the Greenwood Tree*.

The weather for the national holiday is an obvious case of sympathetic background : it favours Farfrae's show. As a result of his visit to the soothsayer Henchard backed bad weather, lost and then cut his losses, whereas had he held his stocks for a while he would at least have broken even. " The fact was, that no sooner had the sickles begun to play than the atmosphere suddenly felt as if cress would grow in it without other nourishment " (XXVII, 217). There is something more than mere sympathetic background in the weather on these occasions, however. It is as if nature is taking an active part in the story, ranged on Farfrae's side, with a malignant delight in Henchard's discomfiture.

The river is a mournful influence in the story (the word " influence " came spontaneously). The town's unfortunates go to brood over the one of its two bridges that suits with their station. Henchard interprets the music of the waters (XLI, 339). Life ahead of him is " as darkness itself ", as he goes to " the dark shapes of the Ten Hatches ", where the noise of the waters is loudest. " After night-fall human beings were seldom found going that way, the path leading only to a deep reach of the stream called Black-water, and the passage being dangerous." (Elsewhere the river is called " the Schwarz-wasser of Casterbridge ".) It is here that Henchard comes intending to make the pool his death-bed, the dark shade of the river suiting with the leaden gloom of his soul. And when the " man of character " actually does die, it is in a derelict cottage held up by the ivy on its walls.

Characters

Hardy is a great novelist because he is an interpreter of character. The chief people in this country market-town are very much alive, and we feel that we should know them if we met them in one of the Casterbridge streets. In his diary for 22nd January, 1886, Hardy wrote,

' The Mayor of Casterbridge ' begins to-day in ' The Graphic Newspaper ' and ' Harper's Weekly '.—I fear it will not be so good as I meant, but after all it is not improbabilities of incident but improbabilities of character that matter.

It is not the story (what happens) that gives the main interest to *The Mayor of Casterbridge* (or any other novel), but the characters. The plot bears the same relation to the characters as the steel girders of the framework to the architecture of a finished building.

Henchard

' He overpowers me ! '

Henchard dominates *The Mayor of Casterbridge* as Heathcliff does *Wuthering Heights*.* Into him Hardy has thrown his whole strength. He makes a profound impression : even Farfrae and Elizabeth are slight by comparison. Six feet one and a half inches without his shoes, he rises head and shoulders above everybody else, literally and metaphorically. That he is a man " of fine figure " is the first thing we are told about him in the clear description in the second paragraph of the book. He is heavily-built, has a " stronglytraced " face, " strong " eyes and a square jaw. A man to be noticed anywhere.

* An interesting comparison may be made also between *The Mayor of Casterbridge* and *Les Misérables*. Jean Valjean has the same doggedness and determination as Henchard, does well in business and becomes Mayor, but *he* is opposed by the law—Javert. (Incidentally, the court scenes in the two stories are very similar.)

It is characteristic of Hardy to begin his stories on a road along which the chief characters are moving. Our first impression of Henchard is of a man who has grown tired of his wife and is walking alongside her, rather than with her, in an " atmosphere of stale familiarity." But he is not unkind, and " gives way to her representations " when she says that she prefers furmity. to " good home-brewed beer, ale, and cyder ". We soon see why she " preferred " it. His weakness for strong drink is well known to her, and she is trying to steer him away from it. Yet " he had been given to bouts [of drinking] only ", says Hardy, " and was not a habitual drunkard ". *The Mayor of Casterbridge* is full of irony. Here is the first example, that his wife's success in persuading him to go into the furmity tent should indirectly lead to his selling her. There presided the furmity woman, that "haggish creature " who " slowly stirred the contents of the pot ", like one of the witches in *Macbeth*, later to reappear and drag him to his doom.

Next morning in his right mind he is smitten with remorse at his action of the night before. Note, however, that his first impulse is to blame his wife, not himself. " Seize her, why didn't she know better than bring me into this disgrace ! " This shows his sense of guilt.

Hardy tells us that " there was something fetichistic in this man's beliefs ". The very form of his self-imposed oath is fetichistic—not for ever, but for the corresponding term of years that he has lived. Similarly, when he sends help to his wife by Elizabeth-Jane, he sends her *five guineas*. His method of waiting day by day for the end of the twenty-one years and then " busting out drinking " is more fetichistic still. His strength of character is shown in the way that he kept his oath, as an act of redemption. No matter what anyone said or did he would not go back on his word. " He've strong qualities that way ", and whether he is the only abstainer or not makes no difference. But his abstinence is fetichistic. He is not happy at the mayoral banquet. His glass of water is there not because he wishes it, but because that is what he must have in despite of himself. " I have kept my oath ; and though, Farfrae, I am sometimes that dry in the dog days that I could drink a quarter-barrel to the pitching, I think o' my oath, and touch no strong drink at all." Whatever Mr. Henchard does he does thoroughly.

There looks something fearsome about Henchard even
in his merry moments. His occasional great bursts of
laughter repel rather than attract : he has no geniality.
He indulges " in an occasional loud laugh ", but " that
laugh was not encouraging to strangers ". Lucetta refers to
his " grim way " of making love. " There was temper
under the thin bland surface " of his skin—" the temper
which, artificially intensified, had banished a wife nearly a
score of years before " (V, 41). But he manages to control
himself, " and he drank from his tumbler of water as if to
calm himself or gain time ". Similarly, when the boys call
poor Mrs. Henchard " The Ghost ", " his face would darken
with an expression of destructiveness towards the speakers
ominous to see ; but he said nothing ". His appearance
after the eighteen years since he last saw her is given in
Chapter V, pp. 36-37.

The hay-trusser whose step into Weydon-Priors in the
early days spoke of " a dogged and cynical indifference "
has shown amazing energy and determination since. " He
worked his way up from nothing when 'a came here ; and
now he's a pillar of the town." He is naturally proud of his
success, and at the mayoral dinner tells " a story of his hay-
dealing experiences, in which he had outwitted a sharper
who had been bent upon outwitting him ". His life as a hay-
trusser was spent in contact with mother earth, and he
seems to have imbibed from her a primitive strength based
on natural impulses unassociated with reason. " Though
under a long reign of self-control he had become Mayor and
church-warden and what not, there was still the same unruly volcanic stuff beneath the rind of Michael Henchard
as when he had sold his wife at Weydon Fair " (XVII, 129).
He has " quitted the ways of vulgar men ", but is still the
same " vehement gloomy being ", who has gained wealth
and power, but not " light to guide him on a better way ".
Nor, indeed, good sense ; the richest, busiest doctor seems
to him to be the best.

So he is still a creature of impulse, and on the spur of
the moment takes Farfrae (who reminds him of his brother)
to him, although he has an interview with another candi-
date for the managership pending. " The face of Mr.
Henchard beamed forth a satisfaction that was almost
fierce in its strength. ' Now you are my friend ! ' he

exclaimed ... ' I am the most distant fellow in the world
when I don't care for a man,' he said. ' But when a man
takes my fancy he takes it strong.' " He overdoes his
welcome in rather ridiculous fashion—" Now I am sure you
can *eat another breakfast*? " And at this second breakfast
he heaps " the young Scotchman's plate to a prodigal ful-
ness ". He never pauses to consider for the best. " He
would not rest satisfied till Farfrae had written for his lug-
gage from Bristol, and despatched the letter to the post-
office. When it was done *this man of strong impulses*
declared that his new friend should take up his abode in his
house—at least till some suitable lodgings could be found."
And Farfrae " saw that his friend and employer was a man
who knew no moderation in his requests and impulses, and
he yielded gracefully ", and consented to have supper with
him against his own will. (" Now you shall ! I am determined on't.") Farfrae wonders at " the suddenness of his
employer's moods " as Henchard grabs him with a " tiger-
ish affection " and " impetuous cordiality ". " Yes ", says
Mrs. Henchard, " I am thinking of Mr. Henchard's sudden
liking for that young man. *He was always so* " (IX, 66-67).

Henchard makes Farfrae his new manager on a snap
decision, without any thought for the man who has an
appointment to be considered for the post. It does not
matter about him—the job is filled, and he must put up
with it. " ' Well, you are too late,' said the corn-factor.
' I can say no more '." Henchard rides roughshod over
people without any thought for their feelings—" masterful "
and " coercive " Hardy calls him. No wonder that Jopp's
mouth twitches with anger ; anyone but a saint would have
felt just the same. Essentially Henchard is a very selfish
man.

When his one-time wife comes back he reproaches her
with her implied guilt in getting him into a mess (*cf.* p. 22).
" But—to lead me into this ! " He speaks of " *our* disgrace " (but his affair with Lucetta is classed only as a
" blunder "). It is typical of men like Henchard to take the
credit for their successes, but lay the blame for their failures
on other people. However, he does qualify his attitude
later by owning that he treated his wife and daughter badly.
What he cannot bear is being looked down on. " She cannot
be told all—she would so despise us both that—I could not

bear it ! " (Notice again that he says " *both* ".) So he thinks of a " natural and easy " plan which " would leave my shady, headstrong, disgraceful life as a young man absolutely unopened ". Another quick resolution—" Judge me by my future works ", and he kept this resolution as well as he kept his first vow, and for the rest of her life he treated her well, as he understood it. This again he does in a " fetichistic " way, " with business-like determination ", schooled " into a course of strict mechanical rightness towards this woman of prior claim, at any expense to the later one and to his own sentiments ", " in a dogged, unflinching spirit which did credit to his conscientiousness " (XIII, 94, 95).

At the best of times he leads a lonely life, in the home and outside it. " Damn it all, I am a lonely man, Farfrae." When we first meet him he is walking along the road out of fellowship with his wife ; after the return of his wife and step-daughter he provides well for them (ornately and lavishly, so it seems to Susan), but gives them no companionship. His contacts with Elizabeth-Jane are occasional and formal, and up to the time when she leaves home he is quite unaware of her interests, " of her care, of her endeavours for improvement ", of her " books, sketches, maps, and little arrangements for tasteful effects ". He never knew how she had tried to fit herself to be his daughter. He sees it in a flash—and it is too late. He gave her what she wanted to spend, and that was all he understood—the end of any man's responsibility. Henchard is incapable of things of the spirit, and in addition he is " getting on towards the dead level of middle age, when material things increasingly possess the mind." Of affection and interest there is none : and none from anyone else when her mother is dead. He fails completely to understand her, to which, of course, it may be said that few fathers understand their daughters. Self-centred men lack sensitivity : he cannot discern the reason for Lucetta's lack of interest in him, or what is meant by the niceties of Elizabeth-Jane's behaviour when she is in love with Farfrae. Henchard seems lonely even at a public dinner ; he is not very approachable at any time and in addition is a marked man owing to his vow.

It is common with lonely people, who subconsciously long for human companionship to fill the gap in their heart, to tell new-found friends secrets that they would never think of disclosing to anyone else. This is borne out by Henchard, and on the first day with Farfrae he tells him the secrets of his past life and his present dilemma with two innocent women on his hands. " I feel it a great relief, Farfrae," he acknowledges, " to tell some friend o' this ! " (XII. 92). Later, when he is annoyed with Farfrae, his annoyance imputes wrong motives to Farfrae's actions, and he charges him (or affects to charge him) with taking advantage of him because he knows his secrets. Incidentally, he is not quite truthful in presenting his case, for he says that " Susan looks upon herself as the sailor's widow, and won't think o' living with me as formerly without another religious ceremony ", whereas it was he who first suggested it and pressed it home.

He asks for Farfrae's advice, but only in the hope of support to prove himself right, not because he really wants it. When it does not corroborate his intentions, he as quickly thrusts it from him. " Now what would you do?—I want your advice ", he pleads, and as soon as the advice is given, " ' Never ! ' said Henchard. ' I am not going to let her know the truth.' " Similarly he " shuts up " Elizabeth-Jane's sensible advice (XXVI, 10), although on this occasion it was not sought.

Having handed over to Farfrae the management of his business, Henchard cannot trust his judgment and leave Farfrae to get on with the job, he still wants to keep control, *and in front of the men*. The climax of this comes when Farfrae stands up to Henchard on behalf of Abel Whittle. On this occasion Henchard behaves like a moody, sullen child. After this Henchard's standing with the men goes down and Farfrae's increases. " Henchard, who had hitherto been the most admired man in his circle, was the most admired no longer." His jealousy of Farfrae therefore increases. His views of people depend (as do those of most of us) on his feelings, not on reason. At first he had expressed admiration of Farfrae's skill.

' In my business, 'tis true that strength and bustle build up a firm. But judgment and knowledge are what keep it established. Unluckily, I am bad at science, Farfrae ; bad at figures—a rule o' thumb sort of man. You are just the reverse—I can see that. I have been looking for such as you these two year ' (vii. 55).

Now he despises him for it. The success of Farfrae's entertainment on the national holiday increases Henchard's jealousy. Passionate liking turns to passionate hatred (XLV, 377). Henchard never does things by halves. He dismisses him all at once, without any consideration (just as he had appointed him), to avoid being " honeycombed clean out of all the character and standing that he's built up in these eighteen year ! ", and by so doing he brings on the very calamity that he would wish to avoid. Farfrae does the most sensible thing open to him, and with scrupulous fairness at that. So Henchard labels him " an enemy to our house ", and forbids him to Elizabeth-Jane. As Hardy points out (XVII, 130), diplomacy might have encouraged Henchard to welcome Farfrae as a son-in-law, " but such a scheme for buying over a rival had nothing to recommend it to the Mayor's headstrong faculties. With all domestic *finesse* of that kind he was hopelessly at variance. Loving a man or hating him, his diplomacy was as wrongheaded as a buffalo's." Henchard knows nothing but brute force. He pushes his way through life. Even his letter to Farfrae is written " with a heavy hand ", and he walks across Lucetta's room " with a heavy tread of some awkwardness " (XXV, 200). Henceforth in business it is " Northern insight matched against Southron doggedness—the dirk against the cudgel." Northern insight wins and in time the tables are turned completely, and, still feeling that " honest work is not a thing to be ashamed of ", he accepts employment from Farfrae (or his foreman), and, indeed, is offered accommodation in his house just as he offered it to Farfrae in years gone by.

Although Henchard is hopelessly at variance " with all domestic *finesse* ", he has a strong streak of cunning, witness his second marriage to Susan, and particularly his dealings with Elizabeth-Jane and Newson. He is a man of contradictions, and on that account more, not less, human.

When Henchard told his step-daughter that he was her real father " he showed a respect for the young girl's sex and years worthy of a better man " (XIX, 140). But then his falseness in opening his wife's letter prematurely kills all his joy in possession of Elizabeth. He does everything just too soon or just too late. Notice the phrase " his joy in *possession* ". It was for his sake, not hers, that he wanted her : had this not been so, he might have been disappointed that she was not his, but he would not have turned against her as he does. " He cannot endure the sight of her ", we are told. His senseless resentment against her is based on self-love. " Misery taught him nothing more than defiant endurance of it " : he had not the character to rise above his disappointment and to become finer by the way he met it. As we have already seen from the scheming way in which he restored his wife to her position, he could not stand humiliation, so his daughter she will have to be—*to everybody except himself*. There is something cruel as well as hypocritical in the way he continues this deception of a good and simple girl, even if it was unwittingly begun. And notice again that he does it *for his own sake*, not for hers : it is to save him humiliation, not to make her happy. As it turns out, his consequent chiding of her for every trivial thing makes her very *un*happy.

He decides to see Lucetta. "To feel that he would like to see Lucetta was with Henchard to start for her house " (XXII, 171). Again he cannot stand humiliation, and his pique at rebuff keeps him away until he is just too late once more. This time his sense of injury has harmed only himself, however.

He wants to know the future ; so with him that is to start to find out—he cannot bear waiting to see how events turn out, or to stop and think things over. Impulse and action go hand in hand. As Hardy says, headstrong natures are often superstitious. He goes to Mr. Fall—secretly, however, in the dark on a wet night. He is getting uncertain of himself : his self-reliance has gone : he needs assurance from someone else. When the " curst conjuror's " prophecy is found to have no relation to the changeable weather of this climate, again Henchard cannot wait. " The momentum of his character knew no patience " (XXVII, 218), and he sells out recklessly, whereas had he waited his loss need not have been so severe. Later in the story his superstition saves him from suicide.

The crash comes. " In a strait " Henchard shows the same sturdy independence as before. He will not " sponge on a woman " or accept money from " Farfrae's wife ", though it might have got him out of a tight corner. It would have been against his whole nature to humble himself.

Be it said to his credit Henchard admits the truth of

the furmity-woman's accusation in court. Had he denied it he would have been believed, in fact the clerk of the court unwittingly made it easy for him—" ' 'Tis a concocted story . . . So hold your tongue.' ' No—'tis true.' The words came from Henchard." That same impulsiveness which makes him do evil also makes him do good.

The news sprung on the court by the furmity-woman is the last straw in Henchard's " tottering credit ". And then his name is dragged in the dirt by his firm's failure to preserve " strict correspondence between bulk and sample." But the Commissioner has " never met a debtor who behaved more fairly ". Henchard is much affected when someone praises him. He offers even his gold watch (just as he has caught sight of Elizabeth-Jane), which was a personal possession and was no part of the balance sheet, and when it is not accepted he goes and sells it straightway, and takes the money to one of his smaller creditors who was in poor circumstances. In considering Henchard as a creature of impulse, the student must remember his impulses for good as well as those for evil.

So there he is where he began, a hay-trusser, and a hay-trusser given to drink, as he was in the first place. Life's intervening experiences have taught him nothing : he is back where he started in mind, too : the irony of it when he says with pride—" I have kept my oath for twenty-one years ; and now I can drink *with a good conscience* " (XXXIII, 268). All he has learnt in life is to get a fierce satisfaction out of obeying a momentary impulse to the letter ; he has not learnt to live honourably and do justly, and think of other people before himself (apart from odd impulses). " Self-reverence, self-knowledge, self-control," says Tennyson, " these three alone lead life to sovereign power ",* but Henchard has learnt none of these.

Though only a journeyman he still acts as if he were a man of authority. There is a no-nonsense felling about him, and he is obeyed out of fear.

' I tell ye to sing the Hundred-and-Ninth, to Wiltshire, and sing it you shall ! ' roared Henchard. ' Not a single one of all the droning crew of ye goes out of this room till that Psalm is sung ! ' He slipped off the table, seized the poker, and going to the door placed his back against it. ' Now then, go ahead, if you don't wish to have your cust pates broke ! '

*Œnone.

And go ahead they did, for they knew as well as Lucetta how " hot-tempered and stern " he was. Savage as he could be, however, " nothing moved Henchard like an old melody " (XXXVIII, 310).

The man who can keep an oath for twenty-one years can nurse revenge. " He was not only the same man, but that man, with his sinister qualities, formerly latent, quickened into life by his buffetings." He plans revenge against Lucetta, and almost carries it through, but by an odd twist in his nature he has just enough goodness to recoil at the last moment. A sudden impulse is once more stronger than a calculated plan. Though he could have annihilated Lucetta (and her husband) " in the heat of action ", to ruin her " by oral poison " is beyond his enmity. Sitting there " in cold blood " he cannot do it (XXXIV, 282). He plans revenge against Farfrae, who had heaped upon him the crowning degradation of a public snubbing. Of course, any reasonable person can see that Farfrae could do no other. He will show him who is the better man ! But, by a sense of rough justice, as the stronger man he ties one arm behind him. Then, with victory in his grasp (" Now . . . Your life is in my hands "), he cannot take it. " And now— though I came here to kill'ee, I cannot hurt thee ! " No sooner is the struggle over than Henchard flings himself into a corner " in the abandonment of remorse " ; he even thinks of winning Farfrae's pardon, or, more characteristically, has an " overpowering wish " to win his pardon. A show of superior brute force has made him miserable, and given him a sense of inferiority to his adversary. A man of sudden and uncertain temper, indeed.

A mad lie to Newson (and again a selfish one) is as soon regretted. Just too late Henchard puts on his hat and follows him. Hardy says that the lie was " the impulse of a moment ", " in pure mockery of consequences ", due to " his jealous soul ". These words are the key to nearly everything Henchard did. Then a " leaden gloom " settles upon him. The " sense of the supernatural ", " strong in this unhappy man ", which had taken him to Mr. Fall and helped to ruin him in business, saves him from suicide.

Like all men, Henchard tries to find excuses for his own ill-deeds. He would love Elizabeth-Jane better than a long-lost father could ever do, for instance. Really he still thinks only of himself. Her affection is now the only worth-while thing in life, and he wants to keep it. He cannot share anything with anybody, and finds it hard to play second fiddle. His is a possessive love (see pp. 27-28). " There was a time when his instinctive opposition [to Farfrae's courtship of Elizabeth-Jane] would have taken shape in action. But he was not now the Henchard of former days." His spirit is broken. " She had her own way in everything now. Her word was law ", and Henchard was a " netted lion ". He " was, by original make, the last man to act stealthily, for good or for evil " (see p. 27), but now he watches his words. He is "denaturalized". He dreads her marriage to Farfrae. It occurs to him that he might lay information which would make Farfrae forsake her. But now the thought does not leap into action. Indeed, he shudders from it and exclaims, " God forbid such a thing! Why should I still be subject to these visitations of the devil, when I try so hard to keep him away? "

When Newson comes back there is only one thing for him to do. " And being an old hand at bearing anguish in silence, and haughty withal, he resolved to make as light as he could of his intention, *while immediately taking his measures.*" He always has a trade to go back to. He shoulders his basket and leaves Casterbridge secretly and alone and heavy of soul, a hay-trusser as he came in.

' If I had only got her with me—if I only had! ' he said. ' Hard work would be nothing to me then! But that was not to be. I—Cain—go alone as I deserve—an outcast and a vagabond. But my punishment is *not* greater than I can bear! '
He sternly subdued his anguish, shouldered his basket, and went on.

A sudden sign of tenderness in Henchard comes as a surprise. It is pathetic the way next morning he takes out a few of Elizabeth-Jane's cast-off belongings and a curl of her hair, looks at them and closes them up again. Hardy's villains are always human, not melodramatic monsters. He goes back to the road at Weydon-Priors where " I drank, and committed my crime ", " as an act of penance "— another fetichistic act.

But he cannot get his step-daughter out of his mind. The man who, in effect, had once turned her out of house and home because he could not abide her, had now grown to feel her loss like this. That Henchard is such a mass of contradictions makes him more life-like than a " consistent " character (see pp. 27). Then, typically enough, he makes a " sudden reckless determination to go to the wedding festivity ". Once again there is to be no welcome over a " repentant sinner " (XL, 328). This is the only place in the book where we feel more for Henchard than we do for Elizabeth-Jane. Thereupon he makes his last resolution, which we know will be kept to the letter, " I'll never trouble 'ee again, Elizabeth-Jane—no, not to my dying day ! Good-night. Good-bye ! "

Nothing is left in life for this broken old* man. His dying day cannot be far away. Further existence would be an anti-climax. He is followed to his wretched end by a " poor fond fool " to whom he had shown himself uncontrollable in anger, but whose heart had been touched by his kindness to his mother when she was old and poor. " Anything you did for one of my brothers here, however humble, you did for me."† One good deed, done without any thought of reward, has brought Henchard the devotion of one poor soul who follows him to his death like a faithful dog at heel.

The last we hear of him is what we should have expected. His will is entirely in accordance with Hardy's conception of his character. The harsh independence and grim fortitude and sense of doom in his life speak out in the will written for his death, without any " palliatives of his great faults ". It was " part of his nature to extenuate nothing ", and he died as he had lived, " one of his own worst accusers ". Such is the last word of a life weighed down by the action of a drunken moment.

The most pathetic touch of all is where a goldfinch in a cage shrouded in newspaper is found a little ball of feathers. That is emblematical of Michael Henchard's hopes.

For convenience in study, examples of two main aspects of Henchard's character are listed separately.

Henchard's quick regret for impulsive action.

Sells his wife and is stricken with remorse next morning.
Tells Farfrae his secret and soon regrets it.
Regrets bullying Abel Whittle (also Elizabeth) as soon as it is done.

*So he appears, though actually he is only in his forties.
†*Matthew*, 25, 40. *New English Bible*.

Dismisses Farfrae and his heart sinks within him next morning.

Tells Elizabeth-Jane she can leave home, and retracts his word ten minutes too late.

Puts off visiting Lucetta through pique, and sees his supersession by Farfrae.

Disturbs the welcome to the Royal visitor, for a moment stands his ground, " then by an unaccountable impulse gives way and retires ".

On the point of killing Farfrae he " flings himself into a corner . . . in the abandonment of remorse ".

Lies to Newson, then chases after him, " amazed at what he had done ".

Henchard tells Elizabeth-Jane that she is his child and immediately regrets it, but while the *effect* is similar, the *circumstances* are not. His regret is occasioned by an independent discovery ; the change in his attitude does not spring from his character in the same way.

Contradictions in Henchard's character.

Weakness in giving way to drink : strength in keeping his oath.

Pleasantness and bad temper are never very far away from one another (*e.g.* the Mayoral dinner).

Made Farfrae manager : wanted to keep control in his own hands.

Bullied Abel Whittle, but kept his mother in food and coals.

At the whim of sudden impulses : yet shows tremendous powers of self-control (*e.g.* the oath again, or when the boys called after Mrs. Henchard).

He will kill Farfrae—but *fairly*.

Seeks something desperately, and then gives up on the point of getting it (*e.g.* the ruin of Lucetta's marriage, disturbance of the procession before royalty, Farfrae's death).

Loathing diplomacy, " the last man to act stealthily " (XVII, 130 ; XLII, 348), he yet has a strong streak of cunning.

He hated Elizabeth-Jane as a step-daughter, but came to love her : he loved Farfrae but came to hate him.

He finds excuses for his evil deeds, yet at other times is his own worst accuser.

Farfrae

' He was a good man. '

The interest of the book depends on Henchard. Other characters derive their interest only from their relation to him. Farfrae is the character who influences Henchard the most. Structurally Farfrae's *raison d'être* is to contrast his quiet reserve with Henchard's volcanic eruptions, his business acumen and initiative with Henchard's old-fashioned rule of thumb methods, his slight build, " pleasant aspect ", crispness and charm with Henchard's frightening look and heavy frame. Hardy acknowledges this—" Farfrae's character was just the reverse of Henchard's " (XVII, 131). His appearance is described, VI, 42 and VII, 50.

Not well-off to begin with, he is prudent and economical and puts up at the second-rate inn, the Three Mariners. There he shows himself a good singer and fond of music, modest and unassuming although not shy. It is significant that Henchard, Farfrae and Elizabeth-Jane are all fond of music, like Hardy himself. In business and in private life he treats Henchard well ; Henchard's business prospers under his management and the secrets of his private life are not disclosed. He enjoys life and never feels like cursing the day that gave him birth. As a manager he never envies his employer's greater prosperity. He has more " native sagacity ", as well as knowledge, than Henchard—" You didn't think of it, you see ; and he did, and that's where he's beat you " (XVI, 123). He knows his place notwithstanding, and meets the Mayor's " impetuous cordiality "with " genial modesty ". He is very straightforward and honest and above board. When he sets up on his own he refuses Henchard's customers at first.

He behaves very sensibly when he and Elizabeth-Jane meet as the result of a hoax.

' Ay ! Then, Miss Newson, ye had better say nothing about this hoax, and take no heed of it. And if the person should say anything to you, be civil to him or her, as if you did not mind it—so you'll take the clever person's laugh away ' (xiv. 108).

He behaves sensibly and firmly when Henchard plays his bullying act on Abel Whittle (see p. 11).

Business comes first with Farfrae ; he has a shrewd eye for profit, " such a knack of making everything bring him

fortune " (XXVI, 210), and the only time he speaks impetuously is not in matters of love but when his face lights
up as he describes his business dealings.

' Just when I sold the markets went lower, and I bought up the corn
of those who had been holding back at less price than my first pur-
chases. And then, ' cried Farfrae impetuously, his face alight,
' I sold it a few weeks after, when it happened to go up again !
And so, by contenting mysel' with small profits frequently repeated,
I soon made five hundred pounds—yes ! '—(bringing down his hand
upon the table, and quite forgetting where he was)—' while the
others by keeping theirs in hand made nothing at all ! ' (xxiii. 182).

He is fond of his dear native country, that, as Hardy
sarcastically remarks, " he loved so well as never to have
revisited it ". " O no, I don't want to go back ! Yet I'll
sing the song to you wi' pleasure whenever you like "
(XIV, 108). " A man must live where his money is made "
(XXIII, 182). We cannot imagine Farfrae ever going to a
soothsayer.

He is not so practical in his *affaires de cœur*. He falls in
love with one woman (or is captivated by her) when he
goes to see another. To give his heart to Lucetta was the
most foolish thing he ever did. In a story, however, death
can intervene to link him with his real mate. He agrees
with Lucetta's statement (not from the heart) that business
ought not to be neglected " for a single minute ", and when
he was reminded of an appointment in the market lingered
only a little longer. Business came before love even on his
honeymoon, though some might prefer to say that he
showed his devotion to his bride by doing his work pro-
perly, in order the better to provide for her welfare.

He is kind at heart, and takes on a young carter with his
old father whom really he does not want, so that father and
son shall not be separated and the old man left to starve.
Farfrae's eyes are moist as he contemplates the struggle
between love and duty in the young carter's heart, and we
should be wrong in assuming that he engaged the carter
merely to impress Lucetta. He is very kind to Henchard
when he falls on ill-luck, and asks him to come and live in his
own house, and buys his furniture in order to give it him
back. Even Henchard was a little moved and shook him
abruptly by the hand, though it made little difference to
his actions. He gives employment to Henchard and
Elizabeth-Jane, and " a feeling of delicacy, which ever

prompted Farfrae to avoid anything that might seem like triumphing over a fallen rival, led him to keep away from the hay-barn where Henchard and his daughter were working ". In reverse circumstances Henchard would have exulted in it. He is polite to his workmen, and he listens to Henchard's letters as an act of grace, though he is not in the least interested. He treats Henchard less roughly than most mayors would have done when Henchard tries to break up the welcome to royalty.

In return for his kindness Henchard nearly kills him. " ' Now,' said Henchard between his gasps . . . ' Your life is in my hands.' ' Then take it, take it ! ' said Farfrae. ' Ye've wished to long enough ! ' " And even then he does not go and give Henchard in charge. No one can blame him for thinking that Henchard's message about his wife's illness is a ruse to decoy him, having failed in his intention of killing him the first time. Farfrae keeps things in mind : Henchard keeps them on the brain.

Farfrae shows a common-sense attitude to Lucetta's death, especially under the circumstances. " It was inevitable that the insight, briskness, and rapidity of his nature should take him out of the dead blank which his loss threw about him. He could not but perceive that by the death of Lucetta he had exchanged a looming misery for a simple sorrow." In a proper time he returns to the woman with whom he was first enamoured. He shows businesslike provision in the wedding arrangements, and if one band gets tipsy there is another in reserve. He and Elizabeth will live a very well-ordered (and conventional) married life.

Farfrae appears at his worst near the end of the book, in the search for Henchard. He agrees to look for him, for, " although Farfrae had never so passionately liked Henchard as Henchard had liked him, he had, on the other hand, never so passionately hated in the same direction as his former friend had done ; and he was therefore not the least indisposed to assist Elizabeth-Jane in her laudable plan ". But when they are twenty miles from home he wants to give up in order to get back that same night, for otherwise it would " make a hole in a sovereign " His circumstances have altered, but he is the same man in nature as he was at the Three Mariners, and will not spend twopence where a penny can be made to serve, even to look for his wife's step-father; just as Henchard is still the same man who sold his wife at Weydon-Priors fair.

Farfrae succeeds where Henchard failed—in commerce, in love and in public esteem, because he is a more ordinary mortal and has the judgment and common sense necessary in ordinary day to day affairs, the lack of which caused Henchard's downfall.

Elizabeth-Jane

This single-hearted girl.

Elizabeth-Jane's kindliness, charm and equanimity contrast with Henchard's irrational imperiousness and ups and downs of spirit, her selflessness with his selfishness. She is a shy child brought up to know life as a struggle. Her character is restrained. Hardy does not " let himself go " as he does with Henchard. Had he done so Elizabeth-Jane would have detracted from the outstanding impression of Henchard. The " aerial grey " of her eyes is that of her whole nature.

In contrast with the pair who had walked into the story eighteen years ago, she and her mother walk hand in hand into Casterbridge now. She is fond of her mother and treasures the memory of her dead father. She knows poverty, but she values respectability, and does not class herself with " the lowest " (III, 25). In those days there were certainly many poorer. She is glad to act as a maid at the inn, in order to help out her mother's purse. Her appearance is described in detail, IV, 28.

This " subtle-souled girl " takes life seriously, and seems to feel about life exactly as Farfrae does, " that though one could be gay on occasion, moments of gaiety were interludes, and no part of the actual drama". " She sought futher into things than other girls in her position ever did." Her plain, old-fashioned clothes suit her earnest and solemn mien; her beauty " had ever lain in its meditative soberness " (XLI, 338). She is modest and has no delusions about her homeliness and lack of glamour. Gossip has no appeal to her, as it has to most women (XXX, 245).

With prosperity and peace of mind comes development " and with development, beauty ". With ready money at her command for the first time in her life it might be supposed that " she would go and make a fool of herself by dress. But no. The reasonableness of almost everything that Elizabeth did was nowhere more conspicuous than in this question of clothes." She did, of course, get new things, but in good taste, and so she became more " distinctively feminine" and less " impersonally human ". Note the descriptions of her in her changed circumstances, XIV, 99–101 and XV, 109–110.

She attracts attention but feels that she is not worth it, as she is so uneducated—" I am no accomplished person." So she sets out quietly and deliberately, " with painful laboriousness " to remedy this defect. Indeed, she becomes very fond of books. In the same way she tries so hard to cut out dialect words from her conversation.

Elizabeth is ready to fetch and carry for everyone, respects her elders and shows consideration for inferiors, which is one instance of Henchard's exasperation with her (XX, 150) —though not the *cause* of it. She gives soft answers to turn away Henchard's wrath, which she feels the more because she is such a sensitive girl. She takes his chiding so much to heart that it begets in her a nervous fear (XXI, 162). We feel much sympathy for her at this turn of events, the reason for which is quite hidden from her, and which she fears may be due to her own omission or commission. Only on one occasion (that is, before her marriage) does she speak up to him with spirit—" O father ! how can you speak like that ? It is unjust of you ! " And when she leaves her father and sees that at the last moment he regrets her departure, she tenderly adds, " And if you want me badly I can soon come back again."

Elizabeth has much perspicacity and good sense. She can, for instance, see through her step-father's character. " Elizabeth, that silent observing woman . . . knowing Henchard's nature now . . . feared that Farfrae's days as manager were numbered " (XVII, 127). By a womanly intuition she divines Lucetta's love for Farfrae (" this discerning silent witch " Hardy calls her), and " by the ' she ' of Lucetta's story Elizabeth had not been beguiled " (XXIV, 198). " How this woman divined things! " says Hardy in another place (XLI, 341). But she is honest and she is wise, and people's secrets are safe with " the close-lipped Elizabeth ". Neither does she show her feelings, a weakness which can lead to unwary disclosure. Yet there is nothing secretive in her, it is simply " habitual reserve ". Younger than Lucetta, " in manner and general vision she seemed more of the sage ", and Lucetta seeks her opinion as such.

It has been said that Elizabeth-Jane's withdrawal into the background while Lucetta replaces her in Farfrae's affection is unnatural self-effacement, even for a " dear, good girl ". What else can she do, however? She is in Lucetta's service as a companion-help, and it would be unthinkable to this strictly honest girl to work behind the scenes against the interests of her mistress and benefactress, the one who had given her sanctuary from Henchard's unhappy home. And so she stoically " bore up against the frosty ache of the treatment, as she had borne up under worse things ". When she goes to Lucetta's it is with a hope that " then perhaps my father might get to love me ".

She had learnt the lesson of renunciation, and was as familiar with the wreck of each day's wishes as with the diurnal setting of the sun. If her earthly career had taught her few book philosophies it had at least well practised her in this.

It is a cynical view of life to say (as some critics do) that there are no women in the world that good, and one not borne out by experience.

But " the meek Elizabeth " knows when to be firm and to speak her mind. She speaks out not in her own interests, but when evil (as she sees it) is about to be done. " Any suspicion of impropriety was to Elizabeth-Jane like a red rag to a bull." Her answer to Lucetta's attempts to justify her marriage to Farfrae is simple, clear and uncompromising. " There is only one course left to honesty. You must remain a single woman." And when she discovers that Lucetta is already married to Farfrae, " the instant decision of Susan Henchard's daughter was to dwell in that house no more ". Her attitude to life is conventionally proper and respectable. It is her duty to go back to poverty—for more than one reason.

When she hears that Henchard too faces poverty she bears him no malice. She might very well have said, " Serve him right for the way he treated me." That is not Elizabeth-Jane. " She felt quite tearful ", and wished to go into the King's Arms to comfort him. Just then Henchard caught sight of her through the window. It appears to have been

the thought of her goodness and honesty, no doubt re-
inforced by her recent absence from him, that made him
offer his gold watch and purse (" all I've got in the world ")
to his creditors. Not long afterwards when he catches cold,
she goes to look after him, " determined not to be denied
admittance "—when it is for his good, not her own. And
when she sees that " everybody and everything seem
against you so ", she goes to live with him and tend to his
wants. Again, it is for his good, not for hers. " I do not
mind your being poor "—and we know that she means it.
As for Henchard's past ill-treatment of her, " I have forgotten it. Talk of that no more." In this she took after her
father. No wonder Henchard failed to understand her, he
who could nurse a grudge for years.

Henchard expected her to despise and hate him for his
last and greatest deception (XLIII. 356–357). This is still
in her heart when she rebuffs him from her wedding celebrations (and even then she does not know that at first he had
been deceived in her identity). Then she finds the poor
little dead goldfinch, her heart is touched and she sets off to
find him, intending to place him comfortably. Her silence
at Abel Whittle's news of his death is more eloquent than
speech. She reads his will. " ' O Donald ! ' she said at last
through her tears, ' what bitterness lies there ! O I would
not have minded so much if it had not been for my unkind-
ness at that last parting ! . . . But there's no altering—so it
must be.' " Kind and calm and philosophical to the end,
" the quiet Elizabeth . . . appraised life at a moderate
value ". She never tries to get the most out of it, but takes
it as it comes, in a fatalistic sort of way. This was Henchard's attitude, but whereas Elizabeth-Jane takes life's
rubs with calm acceptance, Lucetta " with a natural light-
ness of heart ", Henchard meets them with grim defiance.

In marriage " the finer movements of her nature found
scope in discovering to the narrow-lived ones around her the
secret (as she had once learnt it) of making limited oppor-
tunities endurable ". Change of fortune does not alter her ;
she continues to live for other people and at the same time
to keep in the background, and she values the respect of
Mixen Lane as much as that of the Town Hall. Her philosophy of life is the philosophy of Thomas Hardy, the last
paragraph of *The Mayor of Casterbridge*.

Lucetta

‘ I’ll love where I choose !

Lucetta is another one whose life is dogged by the past. Her kindness in looking after Henchard when he was ill in Jersey, apparently towards the end of those lost eighteen years, led to an attachment which went farther than it should have done, and Henchard was going to assume his wife’s death and marry Lucetta just when Susan returned. Lucetta then might well expect that he would marry her after Susan’s death.

The reader is soon disillusioned about her kindness to his step-daughter when she was “ broken in spirit ”, when in her next letter to Henchard she calls it a “ practical joke ”. “ Do you see, Michael, partly why I have done it?—why, to give you an excuse for coming here as if to visit *her*, and thus to form my acquaintance naturally.” One is led to wonder how far her kindness to Henchard in Jersey had an ulterior motive. When this plan does not work and it appears that the presence of Elizabeth-Jane is keeping Henchard away, she is just as ready to dismiss her.

She employs all the arts of the coquette to marry Henchard. She soothes him in her letters—“ I thus look upon the whole as a misfortune of mine, and not a fault of yours ”, and when she comes to Casterbridge rebuffs his first approach in order to increase his desire to see her. Her vivaciousness stands out against Elizabeth-Jane’s reserved disposition, her sophistication against Elizabeth-Jane’s simplicity. She adopts a theatrical pose for Henchard’s reception, but is not a good enough actress to disguise her feelings, and when a man’s step is heard on the stairs she forgets all about it. “ To heighten her natural attractions had hitherto been the unvarying endeavour of her adult life, and one in which she was no novice.” But when she wants to impress Henchard with her misery, she proceeds to “ impair the natural presentation ”. “ She selected—as much from want of spirit as design—her poorest, plainest, and longest discarded attire.”

When an alternative to the grim Jersey hotel guest has become a possibility, duty has no part in her choice, as it would have done with Elizabeth’s. “ I *will* love him ! . . . as for *him*—he’s hot-tempered and stern, and it would be madness to bind myself to him knowing that. I won't be a slave to the past ! " she bursts out passionately. She would have chosen Farfrae all the more had she known that he would become Mayor and bring her " an intoxicating *Weltlust* ".

But she too is married on a deceit, and the past creeps up and gnaws at her happiness, as we can tell as she listens on the stairs in fear lest Henchard will show her secret to her husband. When that deceit is made known to all the town it kills her.

Unfortunately Lucetta has a weakness for letter-writing which lands her in trouble ; when things are down in black and white they cannot be denied or explained away. " ' Poor fool ! ' said Henchard with fond savagery, holding out the note. ' To know no better than commit herself in writing like this ! ' " (XXXIII, 271).

Lucetta is more beautiful than Elizabeth-Jane (although Buzzford did not think so, XXXVII, 306), but much less attractive a character, and it is a mystery how Farfrae, a fellow of good sense, could have preferred her to his first love. But then, people's choice of marriage partners is often a mystery in real life.

The Casterbridge Gossips

These are the lesser townsfolk among whom the main characters live and move and have their being. Their very commonness brings a sense of reality to the story. They make us feel that the unruly passions of Henchard do not belong to a special world of their own, but to the world which is the world of all of us ; an unusual character like Henchard gains reality from mixing with these ordinary folk

The key to Hardy's attitude as a novelist to simple folk is in an essay published by him in 1888. " The conduct of the upper classes is screened by conventions, and thus the real character is not easily seen ; whereas in the lower walks, conduct is a direct expression of the inner life ; and thus character can be directly portrayed through the act." Upper class society tends to file men down to one stock model ; the lower classes have a fresher individuality. The townsmen in the *Mayor of Casterbridge* have a composite entity as a group, and in addition some have distinguishable personal characteristics. It will be noticed that most of the labouring folk in the novel are old men or women, that is men who are well-weathered and hence who have imbibed the prejudices of their class. Their eyes twinkle as they bring back reminiscences of days departed, and they have a high respect for tradition.

The events of their lives do not go beyond town affairs— town gossip to put it less kindly—and in their little circle of interests trifles are magnified into events of first-rate importance, and they themselves made to appear as people who matter. Their comments are obvious enough, but humorous owing to the way in which they are put.

Like Henchard, Lucetta and Elizabeth-Jane, but in a less interesting way, they accept life as it comes and make the best of it. They are content with their lot, but at the same time glad to see their betters made to look ridiculous. As a class they are simple, garrulous, intolerant, unable to see beyond their own little lives. The chief impression of the furmity-woman on the sailor's visit to her tent is that she is " not a penny the better for him ".

The purpose of the townsfolk in the story is

1. To give the reader information in a natural way or to comment on the story, *e.g.* the information on what a " skimmity-ride " is at the end of Chapter XXXVI, or their comments on Henchard's marriage to Susan in the second half of Chapter XIII. So far we have seen Henchard's mar- riage from his point of view : now we know what every Tom, Dick and Harry thought of it, and it gives the story breadth.

2. Humour and pathos, usually together, throwing one another up by contrast, as in the comments of those round the town pump on the morning of Mrs. Henchard's death. The worldly wisdom of Christopher Coney—" Faith, why should death rob life o' fourpence? " endorsed by Solomon Longways, whose inclination is against Coney's lack of reverence, but—you must face facts, and " money is scarce, and throats get dry ".

The pathos of Mother Cuxsom's last comment, with which the chapter ends, " And all her shining keys will be took from her, and her cupboards opened ; and little things 'a didn't wish seen, anybody will see ; and her wishes and ways will all be as nothing ! " like Christopher Coney's wordly wisdom, emphasises that life goes on just as before, and that Mrs. Henchard's death causes a stir for a day or two, but is really a commonplace event in this mortal scene. It becomes more grotesque when it is spoken by a wicked old woman like Mrs. Cuxsom.

The townsfolk's interpretation of the Christian faith is made to fit their natural inclination, and their Christianity is well bound up with creature comforts as they regularly walk after service across from the church to the Three Mariners, but, on a point of honour, only for half-a-pint.

The way Abel Whittle follows Henchard when he looks " low and faltering ", and cannot be shaken off, is the most pathetic episode in which any of the common people of Casterbridge figure. " You see he was kind-like to mother when she wer here below, though 'a was rough to me." Abel Whittle is a simpleton, but he must have a heart of gold.

3. For direct action or influence in the story, as when the " skimmity-ride " causes Lucetta's death, or Farfrae's opposition to Henchard's bullying of Abel Whittle proves the turning point in his replacing Henchard in the men's esteem.

The reader will be surprised to find how little space in the story the gossips occupy. They crop up only occasionally, outside the church, round the town pump, in the two lower-class inns, but by virtue of these odd appearances they give an impression of the constant atmosphere of life (what used to be called " humours ") in this old-world town.

These labouring folk speak, or appear to speak, a rich Dorset dialect, but it is not really ; it has a flavour of Dorsetshire words so that it gives the *impression* of dialect, but Hardy can never depart so far from standard English as to make the town gossip incomprehensible to the average reader not belonging to Dorset. Dialect in a book is always a compromise—it has to be so to be understood. Hardy was fond of local dialect words, " pretty and picturesque " he called them (XX, 148), unlike his Henchard, who thought that words like " leery " and phrases like " Bide where you be " were " terrible marks of the beast ".

Style

Hardy's style is direct, simple and straightforward, with no ornament or hyperbole. It is a quiet style ; there is no bombast, no straining after effect, no affectation ; it does not dance, it does not bang. The prose is never over-written—there is no elaboration for its own sake, merely to create an impression on the reader. We therefore sense its power. Hardy's is a dignified and disciplined style, admirably clear, smooth and continuous. It is under control, words never run away with him.

Juveniles too easily assume that a book with a quiet, disciplined style must *therefore* be tame and dull. It is a fallacy. *The Mayor of Casterbridge* has many tense, dramatic scenes, *e.g.* in the furmity-tent, in the police court and in Farfrae's loft.

This straightforward style is sometimes strongly rhythmic. Many of the descriptions have a rhythmic flow which, combined with their imaginative selection of detail, gives them a poetical quality. The description of the fresh September morning at Weydon-Priors (II, 16) is an example of this, or of the dawn in Casterbridge (XL, 331), of Casterbridge at nightfall (IV, 31), or by day (XIV, 105), or of the town's two bridges (XXXII). The description of the Ring (XI) swells with a distinct rhythmic rise and fall, not a regular rhythm like the rhythm of poetry, but a rhythm " as of wavelets on a lopping sea, one ever and anon rising above the rest " (XXIII, 181). It is reminiscent of the Bible. Hardy knew his Bible, as any reader of *The Mayor of Casterbridge* can tell from the many references to Bible incidents : not more so than other contemporary authors, however, for in those days all well-educated men knew their Bible and the ancient classics. Incidentally, Hardy also quotes considerably from Shelley in *The Mayor of Casterbridge*.

Hardy usually describes his main characters in one piece, *e.g.* the description of Henchard in the second paragraph of the book. This was the regular method in Victorian novels, *e.g.* those of Dickens. The first description of Elizabeth-Jane in prosperity is the longest in the book and reaches two pages (XIV, 99–101). Many such descriptions would slow up the action, and so at other times people are made alive by emphasis on one or two essentials at a particular moment, and the reader fills in the details from his imagination, *e.g.* Henchard (V, 36), or Elizabeth-Jane (XLV, 377), to choose one example at the beginning and one at the end of the book. In life, when we first see a person we do not notice every little detail about him all at once. More likely we are struck by one particular oddity or individuality, and in time other characteristics accumulate around this one quality. So Elizabeth-Jane (and therefore the reader) gets a general impression of Farfrae when she first sees him in the street (VI, 42), and notices details of his complexion when she sees him a second time more closely indoors (VII, 50). Incidentally, such a method of introducing a character makes a stronger, because a more concentrated impression, whereas the impression of vividness can be lost while the reader is wading through a long description. This more dramatic method is the one usually followed by novelists to-day. Similarly Hardy hits off lesser people in his story in a few strokes, *e.g.* the glazier, " a stout, bucket-headed man, with a white apron rolled up round his waist "—just three homely, realistic details.

The time when Hardy is most undramatic in talking of a character is on the occasion when he refers to Elizabeth-Jane as " our poor only heroine " (XLIII, 353). Here the author pushes himself into the story, and once an author does that the illusion of reality is suspended. The author must keep himself in the background, so that the people in his story do not seem to be his creations. Similarly he sometimes comes into the story to give us information of which his characters are unaware, which is quite unnecessary.— " *Though the two women did not know it*, these external features were but the ancient defences of the town, planted as a promenade." Here this derives from his strong local patriotism.

Whether outdoors or indoors, Hardy's descriptions ring true, from his own first-hand observation. They vary from the description of the rich autumn colours in the gardens of the houses in Casterbridge High Street (IX, 68) to the less salubrious quarters of Mixen Lane (XXXVI, 291–292). Further, they do not appeal only to the sense of sight, the most common sense appealed to by authors, but to the sense of sound as well. " A warm glow pervaded the whole atmosphere of the marquee, and a single big blue fly buzzed musically round and round it. Besides the buzz of the fly there was not a sound " (II, 15). A common enough sound, just the one we should expect to hear under those circumstances at that time of year, as natural as the swallows

darting into the tent the evening before. When the people at a
tea-party sit stiffly silent, we are made conscious of other
noises outside.

All exterior circumstance was subdued to the touch of spoons and
china, the click of a heel on the pavement under the window, the
passing of a wheelbarrow or cart, the whistling of the carter, the
gush of water into householders' buckets at the town-pump opposite;
the exchange of greetings among their neighbours, and the rattle of
the yokes by which they carried off their evening supply.

These sounds outside emphasise the silence within. Descriptions are made real to us by an author's choice of significant
detail. Further, Hardy's descriptions are not just photo-
graphic, they convey the feelings of an imaginative ob-
server, *e.g.* the description of Mixen Lane.

One way in which Hardy's skill as a writer is shown is in
his choice of words : " ' Now ', said Henchard, digging his
strong eyes into Jopp's face " (XXVI, 209) ; " a lonely figure
on the *broad white* highway " (XLIV, 369) ; the chimes
" *stammering* " out the hymn tune (IV, 32) ; " ' Ye see Mr.
Farfrae,' *gibbered* Abel." The greatest writers do not use
long words, but simple words that just fit.

The style is not always at the same level, however ; there
are occasional ugly *clichés*, *e.g.* " He had become Mayor and
church-warden *and what not* " (XVII, 129); " finally
wending his way homeward " (XL, 325). And when Hardy
says that Henchard " perceived the roofs of a village and
the tower of a church " and " instantly made towards
the latter object ", his style descends to bathos. On the
whole, however, the writing shows care and craft.

While considering Hardy's choice of words it should be
noted how accurate are his technical terms from music and
architecture, in both of which he had special training (see
pp. 5 and 6).

A sense of reality is given by little circumstantial details.

It was on *a Friday evening*, near *the middle of September*, and *just
before dusk*, that they reached *the summit of a hill within a mile of the
place they sought*. There were *high-banked hedges* to the *coach-road*
here, and they mounted upon *the green turf* within, and sat down.

Such details help to give clearer definition to the picture in
the reader's mind, and when they are " remembered " by
the narrator it seems to give all the reality of fact. So the
yellow hammers " flitted about the hedges *with straws in*

their bills " (II, 16), Henchard walked on to a lane " *a good mile* " away, Elizabeth noiselessly pushed open the door " *with the edge of the tray* ", and downstairs " the *black* settle " projected " endwise from the wall within the door " (VIII, 57). The only lodgings fit for Susan and her daughter are " *those over the china-shop in High Street* " (XI, 85). These are just a few examples from the early chapters ; the student will find many more. Too many of such details would clutter up the story and impede the reader so that he could not move on freely. A judicious use of them gives the truth of fact to fiction.

The dialogue is easy and natural, that of the lower classes being stiffened with racy Dorset words. The banal conversation of uneducated labourers in real life is boring, however. Hardy does not reproduce specimen town gossip, he prunes it and gives a *selection*, as he does with the actual vocabulary (see p. 44).

Attention has already been given elsewhere (pp. 11–12) to the sense of pattern and proportion in the structure of the book. In particular things too Hardy shows care. Nowhere does he say that the second Elizabeth-Jane is Henchard's daughter : it is we who assume it (as Henchard did). When we look back we see that hints are given that she is not (*e.g.* XIV, 101–102). Notice too how the young lovers in the market-place, in the story for only two pages, act as a foil to Lucetta and Farfrae (see p. 12).

The use Hardy makes of contrast is also dealt with elsewhere (including the section on the various characters of the novel).

Hardy's humour generally has a sarcastic turn.—" Everybody applauded the Mayor's proposed entertainment, especially when it became known that he meant to pay for it all himself " (XVI, 118). The speech, actions and outlook of the rustics are responsible for practically all the humour of the book (see p. 43), which is usually unconscious on their part. There is poor Abel Whittle, in the days before alarm clocks, tying a string round his toe and leaving the other end dangling out of the window in the hope that a good friend would pull it in time in the morning. And his fellow-workmen advance " their customary eleven o'clock pint to half-past ten " on an unexpected holiday in Casterbridge, " from which they found a difficulty in getting back to the proper hour for several days " (XXXVII, 302).

The Mayor of Casterbridge is pathetic throughout (see pp. 14–15, 43–44), and one has a feeling that the only purpose of the humour is to make the pathos more powerful by contrast. Even the Abel Whittle incident just referred to has its pathetic side, *because it is Abel*. It might be completely humorous with anybody else.

Hardy makes much use of similes in his telling of the story. Most are from various aspects of nature. Here are a few listed and arranged for convenience.

" The sun shone in at the door upon the young woman's head and hair, which was worn loose, so that the rays streamed into its depths as into a hazel copse " (IV, 28). (Hardy is very sensitive to the beauty of a woman's hair.) In a more gigantic way Henchard is said to move " like a great tree in a wind ". Hardy must have been fond of this comparison, for he uses it twice more (XXII, 175 ; XXXVIII, 312).

The brightness of Henchard's appearance as a young man (contrasted with his indifference to his dress after his fall) is conveyed by comparisons with flowers (XXXII, 262).

" Innumerable tawny and yellow leaves skimmed along the pavement, and stole through people's doorways into their passages, with a hesitating scratch on the floor, like the skirts of timid visitors " (IX, 65). This simile seems to give life to the fluttering leaves (in those days women's skirts dragged along the ground). And this one to the air. " The atmosphere suddenly felt as if cress would grow in it without other nourishment. It rubbed people's cheeks like damp flannel when they walked abroad " (XXVII, 217).

Rather grotesque comparisons are where the sun is compared to " a drop of blood on an eyelid " (see p. 20), or the shadow on the wall to " a red-hot cauliflower " (XXXVI, 290).

No one would think that Elizabeth could be compared to a watch-dog. But as part of " a new idea " it becomes appropriate (XXIII, 188).

The quaffing choir are dignified by Hardy's comparison of their half-pint cups to " the monolithic circle at Stonehenge " (XXXIII, 264).

Some descriptions owe their force to their similes, *e.g.* that of the savage bull (XXIX, 235).

From time to time comes a simile from Hardy's reading, in English or classical story, *e.g.* John Gilpin (XXX, 243), or Juno's bird (XLII, 347).

Occasionally the similes are ordinary, not to say hackneyed, *e.g.* " like a red rag to a bull " (XXX, 246), " like a lightning flash " (XI, 82), " as common as blackberries " (XVI, 118), " his diplomacy was as wrongheaded as a buffalo's" (XVII, 130). Comparisons of Henchard to a lion or a ruin could be commonplace, but Hardy gives them point by the adjectives—" like a *fangless* lion " (XLIII, 354) or " a *dark* ruin " (XLIV, 372).

Hardy makes less use of metaphors, but they can be vivid and appropriate, as when Mixen Lane is called " this mildewed leaf in the sturdy and flourishing Casterbridge plant " (XXXVI, 292).

NOTES

Chapter I

An out-of-work hay-trusser and his wife and little child are approaching the village of Weydon-Priors after a long day's tramp. Man and woman walk in " stale familiarity " without a word to each other. In the village they find that it is Fair Day, and there are plenty of booths about. They enter one for refreshment. The hay-trusser gets more and more talkative, more and more fuddled, and finally, in a half-drunken state, he sells his wife (with the child) to a sailor for five guineas.

fustian, of coarse-textured cotton cloth (but not as coarse as corduroy, and not ribbed).

tanned, *i.e.* leather.

wimble, gimlet or auger.

breves. The longest notes used in music (as opposed to quavers, which are short).

journeymen, workmen, *lit.* those hired out for the day (Fr. *journée*).

thimble-riggers, conjurers, referring to the trick in which the performer concealed (or pretended to conceal) a pea under one of three small cups (thimbles), the onlookers being invited to guess under which of the three it was to be found.

readers of Fate, *i.e.* fortune-tellers.

Furmity. A drink of which the main ingredient was wheat (without its husk), boiled in milk. Other ingredients are mentioned at the bottom of p.5, *M.o.C.*

Hear. Indicating the vendor's lack of education.

laced, flavoured (with spirits).

maelstrom. A celebrated whirlpool off the coast of Norway, hence any resistless, overpowering force.

begad. An oath (*lit.* by God).

Scripture history. Probably referring to Abram separating from Lot (*Genesis* XIII, 8–12).

staylace, laced corsets.

'vation, *i.e.* salvation.

rheumy, snuffling, like a person with a cold. Previously he was said to have " a damp voice. " It does not mean rheumatic.

be-right, indeed, (by rights).

od. Shortened from " God, " to the uneducated mind an ingenious way of avoiding profanity.

'a, he.

keacorn, throat (dialect).

the great trumpet, *i.e.* of the Judgment Day.

the maid, *i.e.* his little girl, Elizabeth-Jane.

Chapter II

Next morning in his right senses, the hay-trusser, Michael Henchard, swears an oath at the altar of the first church he sees, to " avoid all strong liquors " for twenty-one years. He immediately starts searching for his wronged wife and child, but " weeks counted up to months, and still he searched on ". He learns at a seaport that persons answering to his description have emigrated. Thereupon he gives up the search and goes back to Casterbridge.

the Seven Sleepers had a dog. A reference to a part of the *Koran* called " The Cave. "—" So we awaked them. . . . Some say, ' They were three ; their dog the fourth' . . . others say, ' Seven ; and their dog the eighth. ' "
fetichistic, acting like a spell or charm.
sacrarium, sanctuary, the part before the altar.

Revision Questions on Chapters I–II

1.   Describe the group of three approaching the village of Weydon-Priors who set the story in motion.
2.   Give an account of the hay-trusser's sale of his wife, and of his repentance when he came to himself next morning.
3.   How did he attempt to atone for his sin, and how long did he pursue the search for his wife and child ?

Chapter III

Exactly eighteen years later Henchard's wife and her daughter Elizabeth-Jane are again walking the highroad into Weydon-Priors on Fair Day. Her sailor " husband " has been drowned, and mother and daughter are both dressed in mourning. Weydon Fair is changed : they find it poorer and smaller. But the furmity woman is still there, although fallen on evil days. From her Susan learns that Henchard was at Casterbridge twelve months after he sold his wife. So thither Susan determines to go.

withy, made of small thin branches, *e.g.* of a willow.
stuff, of coarse material, usually woollen.
highfliers, swings set in a frame.
furmity. See note p. 51.
soi-disant, self-styled (Fr.).

Chapter IV

Briefly, the story of Susan Henchard's life as the " wife " of Newson.

Mother and daughter arrive in Casterbridge at nightfall. A description of the town. They " bent their step instinctively " to where " music was playing ".

Falmouth. A fishing town in South Cornwall.

in the Newfoundland trade, *i.e.* as a sailor. Newfoundland is an island off the Gulf of St. Lawrence, Canada.

carking, distressing, harassing.

glazings, pieces of glass set in a frame.

coomb, hollow.

champaign, open, level country.

dimity, a kind of cotton fabric.

of brick-nogging, with bricks, instead of plaster, between wooden beams.

bill-hooks, hedge-cutters.

mattocks, tools for loosening hard ground, like a spade with a blade smaller than that of a spade set nearly perpendicular to the shaft, and brought down on the soil towards the user.

butter-firkins, measures of 56 lb. weight of butter.

seed-lips, seed baskets.

pattens, wooden-soled shoes, with rings or bars of iron under the wood to keep them out of the mud.

a grizzled church. Hardy is thinking of St. Peter's, Dorchester, the town's largest and most ancient church. The word " grizzled " adds that touch of genius to the description.

case-clocks, clocks in cases, *i.e.* permanent cases, of glass or wood or stone or marble.

Sicilian Mariners' Hymn. No. 765 in the *Methodist* (1933) *Hymn-Book*. There is also a variation in the revised *Hymns Ancient and Modern* (No. 410). It is interesting to note that the chiming of hymn-tunes has been resumed at St. Peter's on Sunday evenings.

manna-food. Food miraculously supplied to the Israelites in their journey through the Wilderness (*Exodus*, XVI, 14–15).

swipes, thin beer.

growed wheat, *i.e.* wheat in which the embryo had just started to grow, absorbing some of the wheat in the ear, but it had not grown enough for any sign of this to be visible outside (except to the very skilled eye).

plim, swell.

CHAPTER V

The music is coming from outside the King's Arms, and through the window can be seen Henchard, Mayor of Casterbridge, in the chair at " a great public dinner ". Wine is flowing, but Henchard's glass is filled with water.

'The Roast Beef of Old England.' A stirring early-eighteenth-century song by Henry Fielding (music by Leveridge).

the King's Arms. Still the leading hotel of Dorchester.

fall, veil. In those days ladies wore black muslin or lace veils attached to their hats, which they pulled down over their faces when walking abroad, attaching them under the chin. Modesty demanded that they should not show their faces.

akin to a coach, *i.e.* related to a man wealthy enough to have a coach.

rummers, large glasses.

'a. See note p. 51.

banded, pledged, bound.

as stern . . . Jews. This might refer to one or two events in the Old Testament, *e.g. Exodus*, XXXII, 15–19.

to-year, *i.e.* this year (*cf.* to-day).

list, streak—the close, dense streak seen in heavy bread (d.).

CHAPTER VI

A young man of " remarkably pleasant aspect " joins the group outside the window. He pricks up his ears at hearing the people talk of corn and bread, and sends a note to Henchard. Later that night Henchard goes to see him at The Three Mariners. Henchard's wife and Elizabeth-Jane have also decided to stay there.

carpet-bag, small travelling-bag, so called because made of a thick woollen fabric like carpeting.

the Three Mariners. There is still a hotel of this name below the King's Arms in the main street of Dorchester, though it is not the same building as at the time of this story.

flexuous, pliable, with twists and turns.

holland, a kind of linen (first made in Holland).

ventricles, the two cavities of the heart.

yard of clay, *i.e.* long clay pipe.

a four-centred Tudor arch. The most noticeable feature of a Tudor residence outside is the broad low arch of the gate-house, and inside the wide arch of the fire-places. Tudor arches are generally four-centred, so:

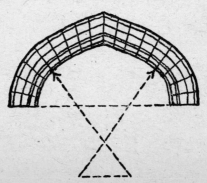

Chapter VII

At the Three Mariners Elizabeth-Jane and her mother
are accommodated in the next room to the young stranger,
in this chapter known to be one by the name of Farfrae,
and can hear everything that goes on there. Henchard
comes to see him, and he shows Henchard a way to improve
his bad corn. Henchard insistently offers him the post of
his corn manager, but he continues firm in refusal, as he
wants " to see the warrld ", and has made up his mind
to go to America.

Before they part Henchard declines a drink of ale, saying
that he is under a vow not to touch it on account of a deed
" which I shall be ashamed of to my dying day ". It would
appear from his words that it is sometimes an effort for
him.

four-posters, *i.e.* large old-fashioned beds, so called because they
had four posts at the corners from which to hang the curtains that
surrounded them.

twelve-bushel strength. Referring to the amount of barley
to make a measure of the ale.

without, *i.e.* outside.

conjured, invoked, appealed to, almost compelled.

corren. The spelling in this paragraph reproduces the newcomer's Scots accent.

Bristol. The great port for America, as important as Liverpool
until the mid-nineteenth century.

quag, *i.e.* quagmire, metaphorically a slough of despond.

refrigerating, cooling, by an ice-safe perhaps, but not by a
refrigerator as we understand it.

science, mathematics, perhaps abstract knowledge in general.

the dog days, *i.e.* the hottest part of the year, in July and early
August (actually 3rd July to 11th August), when the dog-star rises
and sets with the sun.

pitching, *i.e.* of the hay on to the hay-cart or hay-stack (with a
pitchfork).

Chapter VIII

The Scotsman makes a good impression amongst the
" locals " in The Three Mariners. He gives a few songs to
the assembled company. Elizabeth-Jane in particular takes
to him ; " he seemed to feel exactly as she felt about life ".

wheel ventilator. Made to revolve by the wind.

It's hame. . . . An old Jacobite song.

fain, glad, happy.

Annan Water. The River Annan, which flows into Solway Firth.

bands, fiddle strings.

Danged, damned (d.).

a dying fall, a sound or cadence slowly passing away. Perhaps a reminiscence of Shakespeare's *Twelfth Night*, I.i.4.

lammigers, lame folk (d.).

cust, cursed (d.).

rebelled . . . Gallows Hill. This is the survival in the popular mind of the Civil War, in which Dorchester supported the Parliamentary cause, and of Judge Jeffrey's " Bloody Assize " in Dorchester, 1685, after the suppression of Monmouth's rebellion, when nearly 300 people were sentenced to death.

bruckle, brittle, *i.e.* unsure, untrustworthy.

under-thoughts. As we might say, " subconscious wanderings." in his speech.

Botany Bay. The first penal settlement in Australia, near the modern Sydney.

ballet. For " ballad ".

' O Nannie '. " O Nanny, wilt thou gang with me ", probably an English song by Bishop Percy, editor of the famous *Reliques of Ancient English Poetry*, and taken over by the Scots.

' Auld Lang Syne '. A song Burns took down (and improved) " from an old man's singing", and since used as a farewell song at parties throughout the English-speaking world.

chine, ridge of wood round the bottom.

animalcules, small animals.

" gaberlunzie ", strolling beggar.

Arthur's Seat. A hill in Edinburgh.

chiney, *i.e.* china.

an old ditty. An adaptation of the first stanza of Burns's song *Bonnie Peg*, beginning, " As I came in by our gate end ".

CHAPTER IX

Next morning, after some deliberation, Elizabeth-Jane's mother sends her with a note to Mr. Henchard. What Casterbridge looks like early on market-day. Opening Mr. Henchard's office door she sees not him but Farfrae, who has changed his mind and become Henchard's manager.

St. Peter's. Inside is a plan of the church drawn by Thomas Hardy, " for John Hicks Architect ", at the age of 16 (dated " Aug 4th 1856 ").

' bloody warriors '. A local popular name for wall-flowers.

chassez-déchassez. The name of a French dance with a to and fro movement right and left.

Terpsichorean figures, dance figures. Terpsichore was the Greek goddess of dance and song.

in romantic lore. Actually in Scott's *Lay of the Last Minstrel*, Cantos VII, VIII and IX.

metropolitan. Not used literally: it simply means " town ".

netting, making or repairing the netting.

fish-seines, large fishing nets.
staddles, supports.
Flemish ladders, ladders slightly narrowing towards the top.

CHAPTER X

Elizabeth is received in kindly fashion by Mr. Henchard, and he writes a note to her mother arranging to meet her that night. He encloses five guineas in the envelope.

like the quicker cripple at Bethesda. See *St. John*, V, 2–7.
rouge-et-noir, red and black (Fr.). See the description of Henchard's countenance as Elizabeth entered.
Pembroke tables. Tables having four fixed legs and two hinged side-tables supported by legs hinged to the central part.
Family Bible. A large Bible with a page at the front for recording the family " tree. "
'Josephus '. A Jewish historian (A.D. 37–95), whose *History of the Jewish War* and *Antiquities of the Jews* contain much valuable historical material bearing on the events of the Bible.
' Whole Duty of Man '. An anonymous devotional work (1658) which had immense popularity. Perhaps by Richard Allestree. It was considered proper to have these three books in the house.
fluted, grooved.
Chippendale and Sheraton. Chippendale was a Worcestershire cabinet-maker who set up for himself in London in the reign of George I, and whose designs for chairs became famous. Sheraton, in the next generation, continued the same kind of design.
the Ring. See the first part of the next chapter.

CHAPTER XI

Henchard meets his wife as arranged. He wants her, but does not want his disgrace to be known. He suggests that she should stay in the town, and that he should court her and marry her. He is very concerned that Elizabeth-Jane should not find out the truth.

The Ring. Maumbury Rings, Dorchester, was used in Roman times as an arena for gladiators and wild beasts. Previously it was the site of a Stone Age Temple, going back to 2,000—3,000 B.C. Between 1700 and 1767 the Public Gallows stood there.
Jötuns. Giants of Scandinavian mythology.
Coliseum. The name of the amphitheatre at Rome, a magnificent ruin.
the sanguinary nature of the games, *i.e.* gladiatorial displays, etc.
Hadrian. Emperor of Rome, and one of the best of Roman emperors. He built the Roman Wall (between Newcastle-on-Tyne and Carlisle) in A.D. 121.

Æolian. An Æolian harp was a stringed instrument supposed to be played by currents of air. The phrase " Æolian modulations " is a reminiscence of Shelley's *Prometheus Unbound* (IV.i.186–188).

> 'Tis the deep music of the rolling world
> Kindling within the strings of the waved air
> Æolian modulations.

In Greek mythology Æolus was king of the winds.
rub, obstruction, difficulty. A metaphor from the game of bowls.
unconscious, *i.e.* of his approach.

Chapter XII

Henchard confides in Farfrae, telling him of his past as we know it and also of an additional complication.

Achilles. The most famous Grecian hero in the Trojan War. He was educated by the Centaur Cheirion to be a warrior, hence book-learning had little part in his education.
espaliers, fruit trees climbing on stakes.
Laocoons. In Greek mythology Laocoon and his two sons were crushed to death by two gigantic serpents. Hardy is no doubt thinking of the well-known statue in the Vatican (with copies in various places) representing the incident.
Apollo and Diana. God of the sun and goddess of the moon.
like Job . . . birth. See *Job*, III, 1–16.
'Od. See note p. 51.

Chapter XIII

Michael Henchard and his wife are re-married after a couple of months.

substratum, layer underneath (*lit.* applied to a layer of earth or rock).
tumuli, burial mounds.
brougham. A one-horse carriage.
cust. See note p. 56.
husband-high, *i.e.* ready for a husband.
zilver-snuffers. In those days the wicks of candles did not break up as they burnt but bent limply over the grease of the candle, and a big smoky flame resulted. Snuffers were for clipping (snuffing) the wick as it burnt.
cow-barton, cow-yard.
doggery, knavery (d.).
She'll wish her cake dough, *i.e.* wish that she had not made it—wish the deed undone.
bluebeardy, *i.e.* murderous. Bluebeard was guilty of many murders in a well-known French tale. The word is still so used.
'en, him (d.).
twanking, whining, complaining.
jumps or night-rail, stays or night-dress.
cockle-snail. A snail with a spiral or whorled shell.

Revision Questions on Chapters III XIII

1. Describe the two women dressed in black who trod the same highroad into Weydon-Priors exactly eighteen years later, and mention the differences the older one noticed in the fair.

2. Tell the story of these two, mother and daughter, in the interim.

3. What was the first impression of Henchard they were given in Casterbridge ?

4. What befell Elizabeth and her mother at The Three Mariners ?

5. Give an account of Henchard's first meeting with (a) his daughter, (b) his wife (after their return into his life). How had he changed in appearance over the eighteen years ?

6. Do you think that the circumstances justified Henchard's deceptive second marriage to his wife ?

7. Give one or two examples from these chapters of the suddenness of Henchard's moods.

8. What have you found out so far about the character of Elizabeth-Jane ? Be careful to illustrate your answer from events in the novel.

Chapter XIV

The great change in Elizabeth-Jane, now living a " reposeful, easy, affluent life ". But she is reasonable and thoughtful, and does not make a fool of herself. The suggestion that she should be called Miss Henchard gains no response from her.

A trick that someone plays on her and Farfrae, causing them to meet one another alone. Farfrae advises her to take no heed of it, " so you'll take the clever person's laugh away ".

MARTINMAS summer, *i.e.* late summer (sometimes called an Indian summer). The feast of St. Martin is on 11th November. The metaphor means that things became pleasant for her late in life.

Georgian, *i.e.* (in this case) built in the reign of George III, belonging to the end of the eighteenth century.

coulter, the iron cutter in front of a ploughshare.

spencer, a close-fitting bodice.

vivâ voce, oral (Lat.), as in a *vivâ-voce* examination in a foreign language. *Lit.* " by the living voice ".

Casterbridge . . . down. This is still true of Dorchester except for a mass of council houses on the western side.

barley-mow, a pile of corn in sheaves.

at executions. Executions were commonly in public in those days, in fact the last public execution in the British Isles was as late as 1868.

as high . . . temple. This is not to be taken literally, but simply means huge doorways.

staddles. See note p. 57.

victorine. Like a little fur scarf, worn around the neck and shoulders.

'**As I came down through Cannobie**'. Apparently another adaptation of his song at The Three Mariners. See note on " an old ditty ", p. 56. Canonbie (*sic*) is a village in Dumfriesshire, just over the Scottish border, but it has no significance, and to sing of any other Scottish place would have given just as much pleasure to this Scots exile.

CHAPTER XV

An example of Elizabeth-Jane's " artistic indulgence " in clothes. She is beginning to be admired in the town.

An occasion on which Farfrae over-rides Henchard in the yard. Henchard shows signs of jealousy of Farfrae, whom everyone thinks the better man, but it is soon forgotten. He often regrets, however, that he had confided to the young man the secrets of his life.

the prophet Baruch. In the *Apocrypha.* " And taking gold, as it were for a virgin that loves to go gay, they make crowns for the heads of their gods. "

Rochefoucauld. A French author, whose *Maximes Morales* (1665) assume that self-love is the prime motive of human conduct.

fretted my gizzard, worried.

scantling, scrap.

moment-hand, *i.e.* minute hand, which, on a pendulum clock twitches every time the pendulum moves.

gibbered, gabbled.

can't hold a candle to him, *i.e.* is not fit to be his servant, is not to be compared with him.

fairing, present (*lit.* one given at a fair).

diment, diamond (d.).

o'wax, of wax-work, *i.e.* handsome, " the best ".

he's the horse for my money, *i.e.* the one that I take to be the best—a metaphor from horse-racing.

sotto voce, in an undertone (It.). *Lit.* " in a low voice ". *Cf.* " *vivâ voce* ", note p. 59.

CHAPTER XVI

On a national holiday Farfrae's simple entertainment far outshines Henchard's elaborate project, and Henchard is so jealous that he dismisses Farfrae from his employ, though he has not the courage to do it directly.

only scrape . . . talents, *i.e.* Farfrae would decide what was to be done, or, to continue the metaphor, would play the tune.

ancient square earthwork. The remains of a Roman camp (known as Poundbury Camp). See plan.

not forgetting his principles, *i.e.* there was to be no alcoholic liquor.

Æolian. See note p. 58.

Correggio. A famous Italian artist (1494–1534) whose soft and delicate paintings are thus so well described by an author with a feeling for art.

stunpoll, blockhead (*lit.* stone poll).

by a lift, *i.e.* by lifting them and guessing their weight.

" chaw ", mouthful.

the breed, *i.e.* of the mice.

honeycombed, undermined (in the sense, filled with cells and having no solid foundation).

' Miss M'Leod of Ayr '. A country-dance tune that Hardy loved when but a child of four years old.

randy, merrymaking (d.).

Jack's . . . master. A common proverb, Jack, of course, standing for a servant.

Chapter XVII

Farfrae sets up on his own as a corn and hay-merchant (but not at first *in opposition to* Henchard), and he does very well. Elizabeth-Jane promises her step-father to have nothing more to do with him.

dark dense old avenues. There are still many trees round Dorchester, and trees still line all the town's approaches.

spencer. See note p. 59.

varden, farthing (d.).

sniff and snaff, *i.e.* consenting to his attentions. *Cf. Longman's Magazine,* April, 1899, " I expect if any young fellow did say ' sniff ', they'd be ready enough to say ' snaff ' ", *i.e.* to fall in with him, agree with him, especially in regard to marriage.

modus vivendi, manner of living (Lat.).

finesse, subtle artfulness (Fr.).

Like Jacob in Padan-Aram. See *Genesis,* XXX, 25–43.

Novalis. A German poet and novelist (1772–1801). Novalis was his pen-name: his real name was Baron Friedrich von Hardenburg. Hardy probably read of him in Carlyle's essays.

as Faust has been described. Again by Carlyle. Goethe's Faust is, of course, the one referred to. Carlyle was an authority on German literature.

Romeo. Shakespeare's passionate lover in *Romeo and Juliet,* who defied parental opposition (and death itself) rather than be separated from his Juliet.

Southron. A native (or inhabitant) of the South.

' Shinar '. The disgruntled old farmer in Hardy's *Under the Greenwood Tree,* where, in fact, Hardy spells the name " Shiner ". Everdene and Darton are also names of farmers in others of Hardy's novels (Everdene a woman).

Bellerophon. A Greek legendary hero who slew his brother and fled, hated by all the gods and avoiding the ways of men.

Chapter XVIII

Mrs. Henchard dies. She leaves a letter, addressed to her husband, " Not to be opened till Elizabeth-Jane's wedding-day."

Antelope Hotel. The hotel still stands in Dorchester, round the corner nearly opposite the King's Arms.

Paisley shawl. A woollen shawl of very fine texture, traditional in design.

spent 'em at the Three Mariners. Public houses were open all day at that time—there were no licensed hours.

'en. See note p. 58.

Gad. A corruption and weaker form of " God ". *Cf.* note on " begad ", p. 51.

doxology. He means " theology ", and even then the word is not used rightly !

Chapter XIX

Henchard tells Elizabeth-Jane that she is his child, and no sooner has he done so than he finds out (from the letter left behind by her mother) that she is not. Next morning poor Elizabeth-Jane accepts him as her father with " open confidence ", but for him the pleasure he has " prefigured for weeks " has turned to " dust and ashes ".

pier-glass, mirror hung between windows.

entablature, the design over the mirror resting at each end on the columns—another architectural term.

sir. This form of address is not so distant as it seems to us: in those days girls, and especially boys, often called their own fathers " sir ".

like the brethren . . . Joseph. See *Genesis*, XLV, 1–3.

concatenation of events, series of events each depending on the other, like links in a chain.

Prester John. A mythical king of an equally mythical Ethiopian empire, who was punished by the gods in the way stated because he tried to spread his conquests to Paradise itself. The " infernal harpies " proper were monsters of classical mythology, with the body of a woman and the wings, legs and claws of a bird of prey, who, pursuing the vengeance of the gods against Phineus (who had already been blinded because he had revealed the counsels of Zeus, king of the gods), snatched away the food from him every time that he was about to eat.

Schwarz-wasser, *lit.* black-water (the German name of a Polish river). In Chapter XLI (340) Hardy mentions that " a deep reach " of Casterbridge's river was called " Blackwater ".

Franciscan. An order of begging friars founded by St. Francis of Assisi.

Chapter XX

Henchard increasingly finds fault with Elizabeth-Jane, over the most trivial things, until her life becomes unbearable.

Deliverance comes from a lady whom she meets by her mother's grave, a stranger to Casterbridge who has just bought a house in the town and who invites her to become her housekeeper-companion.

jowned, shaken up, jolted. The general sense is, " Be damned ".
the Princess Ida. Of Tennyson's poem *The Princess*.
wimbling, boring through with a wimble, see note p. 51.
Hadrian. See note p. 57.
Posthumus. A pretender to the Roman Empire, who was slain in A.D. 267.
the Constantines. Father and son : Constantine the Great, Emperor of Rome from 306 to his death in 337, and Constantine II, who reigned only three years before he was killed in battle by his brothers. Constantine the Great transferred the capital of the Empire from Rome to Byzantium, thenceforward called Constantinople.
avenues of Karnac. Either the avenues of monoliths at Carnac, in Brittany, numbering over 2,700 and extending about two-and-a-half miles in eleven parallel rows along the coast ; or the ancient town of Thebes, at Karnak in Upper Egypt, with a temple and the " Great Hall of Columns ".
flexuousness, state of being full of turns. *Cf.* note p.54 (the adj.).
Northern Lights, aurora borealis.
Austerlitz. After this victory over the Austrians and the Russians in 1805, Napoleon was at the height of his power.
laconism, conciseness, brevity.
leery, exhausted.
getting ready. In the early part of the nineteenth century people could not say being got ready—the construction had not come into use.

Chapter XXI

Elizabeth-Jane leaves home, and is not dissuaded by a last-minute appeal from Henchard. When he hears that she is going to High-Place Hall, the home of Casterbridge's new resident, " he neither moved nor spoke ".

Palladian. The type of architecture introduced into England by Inigo Jones, which became very popular, so named after the Italian architect Andrea Palladio (1518–1580). It is modelled on the ancient Roman style.
Gothic. The Gothic style of architecture had high pointed arches, and included the Early English, Decorated and Perpendicular styles from the twelfth to the sixteenth centuries in England.

pattens. See note p. 53.
'**tailing**', the small bits of corn that get away from the main mass (on to the tail of it).
fly, light carriage, hackney-coach.

Chapter XXII

It is Lucetta, the complication in Henchard's life, who is the newcomer to Casterbridge. She has followed him up now that his wife is dead. She writes to Henchard to tell him that she is in residence in the town, has inherited property from her rich aunt, whose name—Templeman—she has taken. He goes straight away to the house, but she rebuffs him and defers seeing him. However, he does not call the next day, Saturday, and has not called by Tuesday. Lucetta gathers from some words of Elizabeth-Jane that Henchard will not come so long as she is there. Where now is her plan, which had looked so clever, whereby Henchard could come to see his daughter without any suspicion and at the same time could see her? On the Tuesday she gets rid of Elizabeth-Jane for the morning, and sends a note to Henchard telling him that his daughter is out and asking him to call. A visitor is shown in. But it is not Henchard.

mon ami, my friend (Fr.). French was the language of the Channel Islands in those days, and is still largely spoken there.
étourderie, thoughtlessness (Fr.).
postern, back door (usually of a substantial kind).
Miss Templeman. Templeman was the name of a prominent family in Dorchester about 1800. Hardy would no doubt have heard of the Templemans, and this probably suggested the name to him.
boudoir, lady's small private room.
flexuous. See note p. 54.
Titian. A famous Venetian painter (1477–1576), though Hardy probably had in mind a famous painting of Venus by one of his contemporaries.
the weak Apostle. See *Matthew*, XXVI, 73.
netting. An old craft; ladies generally made the netting as the ground material for fine embroidery.
carrefour, a place where four ways meet (Fr.).
switches, canes.
Candlemas fair. Candlemas was a festival of the Catholic Church, in honour of the purification of the Virgin Mary, on 2nd February, so called from the number of candles used. It would appear then that this was a very ancient fair from pre-Reformation times.
cyma-recta, with a concave curve (another technical word from Hardy's architectural studies).

REVISION QUESTIONS ON CHAPTERS XIV–XXII

1. Describe the festivities in Casterbridge on the national holiday.

2. Sketch the events leading to Farfrae's setting up in business on his own.

3. Mention any occasions (in these chapters) where Henchard is made to look small by the side of Farfrae.

4. Comment on Henchard's treatment of Elizabeth-Jane (a) when he thought that she was his daughter, (b) after he knew that she was not.

5. Why did Lucetta (a) come to live in Casterbridge, (b) offer Elizabeth a place in her ménage ?

6. What is said *by other people* in these chapters about Henchard and about Farfrae ?

CHAPTER XXIII

The visitor is Farfrae, come to see Elizabeth. Henchard had sent him a brusque letter giving him permission to see her, if he cared to do so (thinking to be rid of her).

Farfrae and Lucetta enjoy one another's company. " Farfrae was shown out, it having entirely escaped him that he had called to see Elizabeth." Lucetta's emotions " rose, fell, undulated, filled her with wild surmise at their suddenness ".

When the Mayor calls she tells him that she has a headache and " won't detain him ", and when Elizabeth returns she gives her a kindly greeting—for she now values Elizabeth " as a watch-dog to keep her father off ".

switch. See note p. 64.

hyperborean, belonging to the extreme north.

kerseymere, twilled cloth of fine wool.

St. Helier. Chief town in Jersey (and capital of the Channel Islands).

hiring fair. Where labourers offered themselves for hire for the season.

waggon-tilts, canvas coverings of wagons.

Lady-day. 25th March, one of the quarterdays (so called because it is Annunciation Day).

Cupid. Roman god of love. " Dan " is simply a humorous addition signifying " Sir " or " Lord ", corresponding to the Spanish " Don ".

some ark . . . rest. Hardy is probably thinking of the dove that Noah sent out from the ark " to see if the waters were abated from off the face of the ground ", knowing that if the dove " found no rest for the sole of her foot " the waters would be " on the face of the whole earth. " See *Genesis*, VIII, 6–12.

CHAPTER XXIV

The two young women now live from market-day to market-day. " In an emotional sense they did not live at all during the interval."

In the course of this chapter Lucetta sees Farfrae twice, the first time in a colourful dress specially ordered from London. She feels a little uncomfortable, however, for " her past was by no means secure from investigation, even in Casterbridge ".

Lucetta sketchily outlines her past attachment as the experiences of a third person to Elizabeth-Jane, and asks if this person would be doing right to marry another man whom she had met since and liked better. Elizabeth-Jane refuses to judge the case. " By the ' she ' of Lucetta's story Elizabeth had not been beguiled."

star, *i.e.* fate, the stars considered as influencing people's fortunes in life.

raking, *i.e.* sweeping right across.

carrefour. See note p. 64.

horse-drill. A seed-sowing machine. It is described later in the chapter.

seed-lip. See note p. 53.

the Heptarchy, *i.e.* Saxon England (*lit.* seven States).

Charing Cross. In the centre of London.

The hummed song. The first stanza of a Scottish ballad called *The Lass of Gowrie* (see next paragraph), by the Scottish poetess Lady Caroline Nairne (1766–1845).

so that some falls . . . that. See *Matthew*, XIII, 3–9.

" He that observeth . . . sow ". See *Ecclesiastes*, XI, 4.

their shutters. Shutters were invariably fitted outside windows, even of the houses of the poor, in those days, partly for safety and partly to keep out the draught.

rencounter, casual meeting.

CHAPTER XXV

Farfrae and Henchard both call on Lucetta at different times. Her treatment of Henchard causes him " a perceptible loss of power ". He offers to marry her when she will, but she tells him to let things be for the present. He senses that she has decided not to marry him.

" Elizabeth-Jane . . . did not fail to perceive that her father, as she called him, and Donald Farfrae became more desperately enamoured of her friend every day." As for herself, she was quite forgotten.

Protean, readily assuming different shapes, like Proteus, the prophetic old man of the sea in classical mythology, fabled to have the power of changing himself into an endless variety of forms.

'**meaner beauties of the night**'. A quotation from the first line of Sir Henry Wotton's poem *Elizabeth of Bohemia*, where the comparison is developed so—

> You meaner beauties of the night,
> That poorly satisfy our eyes
> More by your number than your light,
> You common people of the skies,
> What are you, when the Moon shall rise?

The poem is in Palgrave's *Golden Treasury*.

Chapter XXVI

Henchard tries to find out whether Lucetta's refusal to marry him has anything to do with Farfrae. He tells him that the woman whom he compromised will not marry him now he is free. One day Farfrae calls when he is at Lucetta's. The two have tea with Lucetta and Elizabeth, sitting " stiffly side by side ". Henchard, however, could not make up his mind whether Farfrae was his rival, and " left the house with a ton of conjecture, though without a grain of proof ".

He appoints Jopp (the manager originally displaced by Farfrae) as his manager, and gives him instructions to " cut out " Farfrae—" grind him into the ground ", which he is only too willing to do. Henchard consults a local soothsayer about the weather. There is a change in the weather, however, contrary to what Henchard is led to expect, and he loses heavily, so that it is rumoured that the bank has stepped in and possessed itself of some of his property. He angrily dismisses Jopp, who vows revenge.

refluent, flowing back.
gazebo. A raised turret on top of a house, built for the view. Another architectural term.
Tuscan painting. From the second half of the thirteenth century painters began to produce less stiff and unnatural pictures and to paint in a more lifelike way. Some of the earliest lived in the then small free cities of Tuscany in Northern Italy, especially in Florence (*e.g.* Cimabué), and are spoken of as belonging to the "Tuscan school" (which later developed into the Florentine school). They painted symbolic pictures of Bible subjects.

But by the side of the later Florentine painters (*e.g.* Leonardo da Vinci and Michel Angelo, 200 years after Cimabué) the work of the Tuscan school looks, as Hardy implies, " stiff ".

the two disciples supping at Emmaus. See *Luke*, XXIV, 13-35.
pis aller, last resource (Fr.).

domiciliation, place of permanent residence, settled abode, domicile.

scarecrow, *i.e.* very faded.

proximately, immediately preceding.

immediately before . . . grain. The Corn Laws, imposing a heavy duty on foreign corn to protect the home farmer, were repealed by Sir Robert Peel in 1846. See the " Extract from the Author's Preface ".

Alastor. An avenging god.

bell-board. A small table which had small bells on it, arranged in order, and each ringer had charge of several bells and had to ring his particular bell at the right time to make the tune. The metaphor means that the fortunes of Casterbridge depended on those of the " adjacent hamlets and villages ".

water-tights, water-tight boots.

' Candlemas '. See note p. 64.

leery. See note p. 63.

like Saul . . . Samuel. See I *Samuel*, IX, 1–24.

the evil, scrofula.

toad-bag. In Dorset in the last century an annual levée was held near Stalbridge, called " Toad Fair ", because a man sold to crowds of people anxious to buy them legs torn from the bodies of living toads. If these were placed in a bag and worn round the neck, it was counted a sovereign remedy for scrofula. This man had evidently bought a supply (which he would no doubt resell at a big profit).

dung-mixen, dunghill. *Cf.* Mixen Lane, the worst part of the town.

Revelations. See *Revelation, e.g.* VIII, 7–12, XVI, 18, 21.

the south-west. Whence the rain comes.

like tin, *i.e.* pale.

Chapter XXVII

Meanwhile Farfrae prospers. An illustration of the way the rivalry between Henchard and Farfrae is taken up by their men. The incident brings Henchard face to face with Lucetta and Elizabeth. When it is over he tries to make use of the opportunity to see Lucetta, but she sends word that she has an engagement to go out. He waits outside her house to see where she can be going at nine o'clock on a September evening. He sees Farfrae come to the door, and they go out together. He follows them into a cornfield, where the reapers are still working by moonlight, and overhears some of their conversation.

When Lucetta gets back home she finds Henchard inside her house, and, before Elizabeth as a witness, he makes her promise to marry him, under threat of revealing their intimacy.

Elizabeth cannot understand the peculiar power that her "father" must have over Lucetta.

conjuror. In its sense of "one who invokes devils".

roasting . . . brew. Both regular practices of magic. Witches were supposed to make waxen images of people upon whom they wished to bring mischief, then to stick pins in them, "roast" them etc., thereby bringing evil to those represented. The witches' brew in *Macbeth* (IV, i) is a good example of "an unholy brew" to "confound" a person.

It may startle some students to know that as late as 1961, at Reigate, Surrey, a summons (which was dismissed with costs) was issued against a man of 72, alleging that he sent a former employee an effigy pierced by a needle, "thereby intimating to him that he had laid a curse on him".

confound. In its old sense of ruin, damn, as in the *Te Deum*, "Let me never be confounded".

Capitol. In all the chief cities of the Roman Empire there was a capitol, or town hall.

zwailing, swaying (d.).

gawk-hammer, awkward, silly (d.).

thillhorse, horse between the shafts.

pot-house. *i.e.* ale-house.

shocks, piles of sheaves of corn.

lucubrations, lamplight studies.

no'thern, (for "northern"), wandering (in mind), incoherent, slightly deranged. A Somersetshire dialect word.

Chapter XXVIII

The furmity woman is charged before Henchard on the bench, and she reveals his past. "And the man who sold his wife in that fashion is the man sitting there in the great big chair." This story takes the town by the ears.

Lucetta goes away to Port Bredy for a few days, during which Henchard makes one or two calls at the house enquiring for her.

Petty Sessions. Courts for the trial of minor offences by magistrates—"simple business", not serious enough to go before a jury (petty=Fr. "petit").

Shallow and Silence. Two foolish country justices, of many words and few ideas, in Shakespeare's play *King Henry IV, Part II*.

ashlar. A hewn or squared piece of stone, as distinct from a rough piece straight from the quarry.

in the country . . . fatness. Either *Psalm* XXXVI, 5–8 or LXV, 9–13.

instinct, Hannah Dominy. Hardy is having a bit of fun at an unlettered country constable. There were many in those days.

wambling, moving unsteadily, staggering.

turmit-head. For " turnip-head ", *i.e.* blockhead.
for her revenge, *i.e.* because she has had her revenge.
larry, commotion (d.).

CHAPTER XXIX

Henchard saves the life of Lucetta (and of Elizabeth-Jane too) from a fierce bull, only to find that he has saved the life of Farfrae's wife. They were married in Port-Bredy.

concatenations. See note p. 62.

with Abrahamic success. See *Genesis*, XIII, 2.

Yahoo. The name given by Swift in *Gulliver's Travels* to a class of animals which have the forms of men but the understanding and passions of the lowest brutes.

the Thames . . . yore. The Thames Tunnel, opened in 1843, was the greatest engineering triumph of Sir Marc Brunel (father of the Brunel mentioned in the note to " an immense engineering work ", p. 75). Toys of the peep-show type were modelled on it, in which one peeped through the tunnel. Londoners may be interested to know that the tunnel now forms part of the electrified line between Whitechapel and New Cross.

Gurth's collar of brass. Gurth, the faithful swineherd in Scott's *Ivanhoe*, had " a brass ring soldered fast round his neck, so loose as to form no impediment to his breathing, yet so tight as to be incapable of being removed, excepting by the use of the file ".

sirocco. The name given in Italy to the dry South wind which has come over the Sahara desert.

CHAPTER XXX

Farfrae moves into Lucetta's house. Elizabeth, a stickler for propriety, is shocked to be told by Lucetta that she has married Farfrae, when (as it seemed to her) she was in honour bound to marry Henchard or remain single.

Lucetta wants her to stay, but " the instant decision of Susan Henchard's daughter was to dwell in that house no more. Apart from her estimate of the propriety of Lucetta's conduct, Farfrae had been so nearly her avowed lover that she felt she could not abide there." She leaves a note for Lucetta, slips quietly out and that very night takes lodgings " in the street in which Henchard lived, and almost opposite his door ".

like John Gilpin. In William Cowper's well-known ballad-poem of that title.

> For saddle-tree scarce reach'd had be,
>   His journey to begin,
> When, turning round his head, he saw
>   Three customers come in.
>
> So down he came ; for loss of time
>   Although it grieved him sore,
> Yet loss of pence, full well he knew,
>   Would trouble him much more.

brougham. See note p. 58.

Ovid. A famous Latin poet (43 B.C.–A.D. 18). The line is a well-known one from his Metamorphoses, " I see better things and I approve, I follow after worse ".

Nathan tones, *i.e.* damning tones, such as were used by the prophet Nathan in condemnation of David for his marriage to Bath-sheba—" Thou art the man ". See II *Samuel*, XII, 1–9.

seines. See note on " fish-seines ", p. 57.

CHAPTER XXXI

After the police-court incident Henchard's fortunes begin to descend rapidly. He is adjudged bankrupt, and Farfrae buys his business. He is, however, very honest with his creditors.

He goes into poor lodgings (in Jopp's cottage) and gives orders that no one is to be admitted to see him. Even Elizabeth-Jane cannot get near him.

the Commissioners. Corresponding to the modern Receiver.

hair-guard, a piece of muslin or hair-crape covering it. *Cf. Our Mutual Friend,* " With his decent silver watch . . . and its decent hair-guard " (II, i.).

Boldwood. An aristocratic farmer of Little Weatherbury in *Far from the Madding Crowd. Cf.* note on " ' Shinar ' ", p. 61.

wimble. See note p. 51.

vitrified, *i.e.* with panes of glass.

sash-bars. For the panes of glass.

window-jambs, side-pieces of window-frames.

arch-labels, mouldings over doors, windows etc., or parts of them ; in particular the arch-label was a small projecting moulding where an arch joined the wall.

larry. See note p. 70.

cat-head, a strong beam of timber projecting from the wall, through which the ropes pass by which sacks are hauled up.

CHAPTER XXXII

Farfrae buys Henchard's house, and he and Lucetta move there.

He treats Henchard magnanimously, however, at the same time keeping in the rear of the benefits he puts in

his way, the chief of which is employment. Thus their
positions are reversed.

Henchard catches cold and is confined to his room, and
now Elizabeth-Jane will not be denied admission. " The
ice was broken . . . and . . . she had reconciled her step-
father to her visiting him."

As time wears on he loses his pride in himself and gets
moody, the rumour that Farfrae is to be proposed for
Mayor particularly making him bitter. In reckless tones
he looks forward to the end of the time that he is bound by
his oath. " In twelve days it will be twenty-one years since
I swore it, and then I mean to enjoy myself, please God ! "
And so Elizabeth-Jane hears someone say, " Michael Henchard have busted out drinking after taking nothing for
twenty-one years ! "

misérables, miserable folk, wretches (Fr.).

Adonis. A handsome youth of legendary story, beloved by
Venus, goddess of love.

journey-work, *i.e.* work as a hired labourer (*lit.* day by day,
Fr. " journée "). See note on " journeymen ", p. 51.

the Prophet's chamber. The chamber of Elisha in Shunem.
See II *Kings*, IV, 8–11.

stock. A wide band serving the purpose of a collar and tie.

Chapter XXXIII

The scene in the Three Mariners on the Sunday afternoon
when Henchard is free from his oath and he can go back
to drink. This is where Elizabeth-Jane finds him.

From what he says to her, and from what she notices for
herself, Elizabeth-Jane resolves to caution Farfrae to be-
ware for his safety.

the Three Mariners Inn. See note on " spent 'em at the Three
Mariners ", p. 62.

the choir. This was before the coming of the organ to country
churches. The music was made by an orchestra, usually in the west
gallery of the Church. Hardy's father was a fiddler in Stinsford
Church Choir (see p. 5).

bass-viols, 'cellos.

the monolithic circle at Stonehenge. The circle of single
pillars of stone marking this famous prehistoric monument. The
penultimate scene in Hardy's novel *Tess of the d'Urbervilles* is set
at Stonehenge.

dramless, *i.e.* without taking a dram of liquor.

Sound A. As the tuning note.

stave, *i.e.* verse (of a hymn).

rantipole rubbish. A " rantipole ride " publicised a man who had beaten his wife. The scene was acted on a cart in a procession, with appropriate verses (*cf.* the skimmington ride, Chapter XXXIX). Hence " rantipole rubbish " was such rough verses as would be sung on an occasion like this.

in the gallery, *i.e.* where the choir sit. See note on " the choir ", above.

Samuel Wakely. A contemporary hymn-tune writer (about 1820–1882).

Wiltshire. Still a much-loved hymn-tune (by Sir G. T. Smart, 1798), the tune to which the Tate and Brady metrical version of *Psalm* XXXIV (1696) is usually set (" Through all the changing scenes of life ").

comminatory, threatening punishment.

Rosalind's exclamation. In Shakespeare's *As You Like It*, III. v. 57–58.

cat-head. See note p. 71.

trap, *i.e.* trapdoor.

Revision Questions on Chapters XXIII–XXXIII

1. What accident brought Farfrae and Lucetta together ? Give a brief account of their first meeting. What difference did it make *at once* to Elizabeth-Jane ?

2. What particular circumstances caused Henchard's bankruptcy ?

3. Do you think that Lucetta was justified in marrying Farfrae without telling him of her past ?

4. Describe the court scene where the furmity-woman was charged.

5. " Small as the police-court incident had been in itself, it formed the edge or turn in the incline of Henchard's fortunes. On that day—almost at that minute—he passed the ridge of prosperity and honour, and began to descend rapidly on the other side ". Give one or two instances showing how he " began to descend rapidly on the other side ".

6. Describe how Henchard saved Lucetta and Elizabeth-Jane from the bull.

7. " Michael Henchard have busted out drinking after taking nothing for twenty-one years ". Describe the scene.

Chapter XXXIV

Elizabeth-Jane, at much cost to herself, gives a vague warning to Farfrae. He makes light of it, but it is not lost. He had planned to help Henchard by setting him up in a seedsman's shop, but is told by someone else that Henchard hates him and gives up the idea.

Meeting Henchard in the market Lucetta (not for the first time) asks him to return her letters. He remembers that they are in his old safe at Farfrae's house. He arranges with Farfrae to call for them, intending to blast her happiness, but when it comes to it " such a wrecking of hearts " in cold blood " appals even him ", and he reads out bits of the letters, but then takes them and goes quietly away.

shoon. The old (particularly northern) form of " shoes ".
siller. Scots for " silver ".
Tamerlane. In Handel's opera *Tamerlano*.
Aphrodite. The Greek name of the Roman goddess Venus. See note on " Adonis ", p. 72.
subscription, *i.e.* signature, the literal meaning—what is written underneath.

Chapter XXXV

Lucetta overhears part of Henchard's interview with her husband. Her suspense is terrible, until she finds that Henchard has not told her secret. She cannot understand his motive in reading parts of her letters without revealing the name of the writer. She writes a note to Henchard asking him to meet her at dusk—at the Ring. She tries to appeal to his pity by a toilette lessening her natural attractions. She had unwittingly half gained her wish by choosing the Ring as their rendez-vous, it " so strongly revived in his soul the memory of another ill-used woman who had stood there and thus in bygone days ". He promises to send her the letters next morning. " ' Now don't doubt me ', he added, ' I can keep my word.' "

toilette, style of dress.

Chapter XXXVI

When Lucetta gets back home she finds Jopp waiting outside her house. He wants her to get her husband to recommend him as a partner to a corn-merchant. She will have nothing at all to do with it.

Back in his lodgings, Henchard asks Jopp to take the parcel of letters to Mrs. Farfrae.

On his way Jopp calls at Peter's Finger, and before long the contents of the letters are everybody's business, though allusive only, and not altogether plain. They are considered to be an excellent foundation for a " skimmity-ride ".

A stranger, who has lost his way, calls at the inn, and contributes £1 towards the skimmity-ride before he goes.

Jopp delivers the parcel of letters next morning, and within an hour its contents are ashes.

dogs, bars which support the ends of the logs in a wood fire.
candle-snuff. See note on " zilver-snuffers ", p. 58.
tyro, novice.

congeries, collection.
Adullam, *i.e.* resort of those in distress. See I *Samuel*, XXII, 1–2.
bibbing, tippling.
spit, a long narrow piece of land jutting out into the sea.
sallows, willow-trees (especially smaller kinds).
You disappeared for a time, *i.e.* in prison.
lifeholders, *i.e.* their lease of their house and land lasted for life.
copy-holders, *i.e.* the holders held no original deeds confirming their tenure, only a copy of the manorial court-roll.
like Ashton . . . Ravenswood. At the very end of Scott's *Bride of Lammermoor,* Ravenswood was riding speedily across the sands, when he was swallowed up by quicksands, and at once his figure "became invisible, as if it had melted into the air". Ashton "rubbed his eyes, as if he had witnessed an apparition ".
swingels. The swinging parts of flails.
blower, a metal plate put over the upper part of a fireplace, so as to draw up the fire.
oven-pyle. A bundle of faggots of wood (ready to light the oven fire).
skimmity-ride, skimmington ride, *i.e.* a burlesque procession to ridicule a henpecked husband.

CHAPTER XXXVII

A Royal Personage is passing through Casterbridge and an address of welcome is prepared.

Foolishly seeking to bring himself into the limelight on the occasion, Henchard is only pushed out of the way by the Mayor, Donald Farfrae, and made to look small.

There are rumours that the skimmity-ride is planned for the same night.

an immense engineering work. There were many such in the West Country in the early days of railways, in particular those of I. K. Brunel, engineer of the Great Western Railway.
since the days . . . George. George III was king until 1820, but he did not *reign* after 1810, when he went mad.
to change horses. Weymouth was a favourite watering-place of George III.
fête carillonnée, festival of chimes.
tilt bonnets, *i.e.* sun bonnets. *Cf.* " waggon-tilts ", note p. 65.
cortège, procession (although generally used of a funeral).
but had not . . . as yet. The railway reached Dorchester in 1847.
unicorn, *i.e.* in the Royal coat-of-arms.

saw that his Calpurnia's cheek was pale. As at the beginning of Shakespeare's *Julius Cæsar*, when Cæsar is in a public place with a great crowd following, Brutus notices that the cheek of Calpurnia, Cæsar's wife, is pale. See *Julius Cæsar*, I.ii.185.

heavily as Pharaoh's chariots. In pursuit of the Israelites. See *Exodus*, XIV, 9.

go snacks wi'en, *i.e.* share his table.

hontish, haughty.

toppered, brought low, tumbled down.

inquiration, inquiry.

pat, fitting, apt.

Chapter XXXVIII

Henchard left a message at his employer's house, saying that he would be glad to see him at the granaries as soon as convenient. He went up to the top floor and when Farfrae came told him that he was there " to finish out that little wrestle you began this morning. There's the door, forty foot above ground. One of us two puts the other out by that door—the master stays inside. . . . As the strongest man I've tied one arm to take no advantage of 'ee. D'ye understand? Then here's at 'ee ! "

The fight moves to and fro, until eventually, when Farfrae's life is in Henchard's hands—he cannot take it. He flings himself into a corner, and Farfrae goes down the ladder. Henchard hears a horse put into a gig.

Later that night Henchard's " listless attention was awakened by sounds of an unaccustomed kind . . . a confusion of rhythmical noises " in the town.

Weltlust, love of wordly pleasure (Germ.).

breaking fence, *i.e.* breaking down the fence, breaking out through the fence.

litter down, *i.e.* put them on clean straw for the night.

'" **And here's. . . thine.** "' The first two lines of the fourth stanza of Burns's famous song *Auld Lang Syne*. " Fiere " = companion.

Chapter XXXIX

The skimmington-ride takes place. Lucetta has a fit when she sees the effigies of herself and Henchard. The doctor says that it is serious. Farfrae is away from home and is sent for.

As soon as the magistrates and constables appear the skimmington disappears into thin air.

kerseymere. See note p. 65.

agape, open-mouthed with wonder or expectation.

cleavers, choppers.

crouds, fiddles.

humstrums, hurdy-gurdies.

lammigers. See note p. 56.

felo de se, suicide (a legal term).

soughed, sighed (as the wind went through them).

fustian. See note p. 51.

like the crew of *Comus.* " Break off, break off ! . . . Run to your shrouds within these brakes and trees," commands Comus, and his " rout of monsters " similarly disappears. See Milton's *Comus,* 145–147.

CHAPTER XL

Henchard cannot rest that night. He seeks his step-daughter, follows her to Mrs. Farfrae's, learns what has occurred, and how someone has set out to meet Farfrae on the Budmouth Road, so that he would be as quick as possible.

But after his wrestle with Farfrae, Henchard had over-heard him say that he would be going to Weatherbury and Mellstock (an anonymous letter called him to Weatherbury —a contrivance to get him out of the way during the skimmington-ride). " But, alas ! for Henchard ; he had lost his good name. They would not believe him." Neither will Farfrae when Henchard meets him on the road from Weatherbury and tries to persuade him not to turn aside to Mellstock but to go straight back. He fears another trap.

When Henchard gets home Jopp tells him that " a kind of traveller, or sea-captain of some sort " has been enquiring for him.

Lucetta dies in the early hours.

off, *i e.* the one on the off side (the side nearer to the middle of the road).

like a less scrupulous Job. See note on " like Job . . . birth ", p. 58.

a well-be-doing man, *i.e.* a man doing well.

inconsequent, unreasonable, inconsistent.

Lucifer. The morning star.

REVISION QUESTIONS ON CHAPTERS XXXIV–XL

1. Describe the interior of Peter's Finger, and the way the contents of Jopp's parcel became common property.

2. How did Henchard try to embarrass Farfrae, the Mayor, at the official welcome to the town's Royal visitor ? Did he succeed in doing so ?

3. Mention two ways in which Henchard plotted at different times to do injury to Farfrae, and show how in each case he could not *quite* bring himself to the point of doing it.

4. Describe the " skimmity-ride " in Casterbridge and how it faded into thin air.

5. Who in particular would you say was responsible for Lucetta's death ?

6. Give an example from these chapters of where a well-meant action turns out ill.

CHAPTER XLI

The stranger who had called at Peter's Finger before the skimmington-ride was Newson, who now pays Henchard a visit, enquiring for Elizabeth-Jane. Even while she is in the house (asleep in another room) Henchard tells him that she is dead. He goes away dejected.

Henchard goes out to commit suicide by throwing himself into a dam on the river. He is miraculously stopped from doing so by seeing *himself* in the water. (Actually it was the effigy of him used in the skimmington-ride.)

Elizabeth gets an inkling of his desperate intentions, and offers to come and look after him. He is overjoyed, but with a lurking fear that Newson will soon return and he will not have her for long.

broke. The old past participle.
socked, gave short, loud sighs, gurgled.
recitative. Musical declamation : union of song and speech, as in the dialogue parts of an opera.
fugue. A musical composition in which short themes seem to chase each other.

CHAPTER XLII

Henchard fancies that Elizabeth-Jane and Farfrae are getting fond of one another. He is uneasy, but is " not now the Henchard of former days ", and accepts her will " as absolute and unquestionable ". " At last full proof was given him." He has one wicked thought to keep her for himself by telling Farfrae that Elizabeth-Jane is, legally, nobody's child, but he banishes it from him quickly.

' in his own grey style '. A quotation from Shelley's *Epipsychidion* (1.55).

muff. In winter-time in those days ladies carried a "muff" to keep their hands warm—a fur cover about a foot or so long, into which they put their hands, walking along with the muff hugged in front of them.

Juno's bird. The peacock.

Argus eyes. Argus had a hundred eyes. Juno set him to watch Io, but Mercury slew him, after which his eyes were put on the tail of Juno's sacred peacock.

solicitus timor, anxious fear (Lat.). A phrase from Ovid's *Epistolæ Heroïdum*.

get a glimpse . . . everyday. The sea can be seen from a hill on the Weymouth (Budmouth) Road about two miles from Dorchester (Casterbridge).

locus standi, recognised position (Lat.).

Chapter XLIII

It is common knowledge that Mr. Farfrae "walks with" Henchard's stepdaughter. Henchard is worrying over what his position will be after their marriage, when he sees that Newson has returned. Thereupon, without hesitation, he gets his hay-trusser's tools and walks out of the town.

Elizabeth-Jane discovers that Newson is her father after all, and finds it impossible to forgive Henchard his deceit.

Then Elizabeth, Newson and Farfrae turn to wedding preparations.

Mrs. Stannidge. See Chapter VII.

pillow. For " pillar ! "

éclat, distinction (Fr.).

Mai Dun. A large (earthwork) fortress of the Ancient Britons, situated from Dorchester as Hardy says, commonly known as " Maiden Castle ".

Via, highroad, path—a Roman word for a Roman road.

knee-naps, leather pads worn over the knees.

Cain. See *Genesis* IV, 8–15.

schiedam, Hollands gin (named from the town in Holland, near Rotterdam, where it used to be chiefly made).

lying, *i.e.* staying.

Chapter XLIV

Henchard goes fifty miles away, but cannot get Elizabeth out of his mind. He hears, by questioning a waggoner's wife, that she is to be married on Martin's Day.

He turns up at the back door while the wedding celebrations are in progress, bringing a little present, temporarily left outside as it is awkward to carry. In due course Elizabeth comes to see the " humble old friend " who is waiting for her. " Oh—it is—Mr. Henchard ! " she says. She cannot love him, and " gently drew her hand away " from his.

So he makes off there and then. " I'll never trouble 'ee again, Elizabeth-Jane—no, not to my dying day ! "

quickset, hawthorn hedge.

ballet-sheet, *i.e.* ballad-sheet. See Chapter I.

pixy-ring. A ring of a different kind of grass, common on meadows and heaths (*lit.* fairy-ring).

centripetal, tending towards the centre (the opposite of centrifugal).

pari passu, at the same pace (Lat.).

without horses, *i.e.* by rail.

mid. For " might ".

waggon-tilt. See note p. 65.

Martin's Day. 11th November.

the drag. An iron shoe fitted under one of the wheels to make it " drag " instead of revolve.

a Samson shorn, *i.e.* a strong man now bereft of his strength. See *Judges* XVI, 15–21.

emolliated, softened.

back-parlour. The full stop at this word in " The Scholar's Library " edition of the novel is a misprint.

bass-viol. See note p. 72.

saltatory, dancing, leaping.

' **the shade . . . upthrown** '. A quotation from Shelley's *Revolt of Islam*, VIII.vi.2 (l. 3245 of the poem). The student will have noticed the proportionately large number of quotations from Shelley's poems.

Chapter XLV

In the first week of her married life Elizabeth-Jane finds " a new bird-cage, shrouded in newspaper, and at the bottom of the cage a little ball of feathers—the dead body of a goldfinch ". It is Henchard's intended wedding present, and from the hour that she realises it " her heart softened towards the self-alienated man ".

She and Farfrae therefore go to seek Henchard, and eventually find him in " what was of humble dwellings surely the humblest ". But it is too late : he has been dead half-an-hour. His last days have been cared for by Abel Whittle, who followed him doggedly out of Casterbridge, because " he was kind-like to mother when she wer here below " They read his will, a piece of bitter anguish pencilled on a crumpled scrap of paper.

Finally, the life into which Elizabeth-Jane is settled. Her

position gives her " much to be thankful for ", but she is not unmindful of the wants of others.

Crusoe, *i.e.* marooned mariner, from Robinson Crusoe, the hero of Defoe's famous romance of that title.

antipodean absences, *i.e.* absences in penal settlements in Australia. Incidentally, the " Tolpuddle martyrs " were sentenced at Dorchester assizes.

half-yearly occurrences, *i.e.* at the assizes, when people were sent to prison.

victorine. See note p. 59.

Minerva-eyes, *i.e.* wise, thoughtful eyes. Among other attributes Minerva was represented as goddess of wisdom, and the context would seem to indicate that this is Hardy's emphasis here.

' whose gestures beamed with mind '. The editor regrets that he has been unable to trace this quotation, and would be grateful to any reader who is able to locate it.

tumuli, burial mounds.

Diana Multimammia, *lit.* Diana of the many breasts, symbolising her worship as the goddess of human fertility.

supinely, *i.e.* surface or top upwards.

wambled. See note p. 69.

fond, silly.

traps, pieces of rickety furniture.

Caphernaum, *i.e.* " darkness ", " the region and shadow of death " (contrasted with the " light " now). See *Matthew*, IV, 13–16.

discovering. In its old-fashioned meaning of " disclosing ", *lit. un*covering.

cunning, skilful, clever.

microscopic treatment, *i.e.* as if looking at them through a microscope.

REVISION QUESTIONS ON CHAPTERS XLI–XLV

1. Describe Newson's visit to Henchard on the morning of Lucetta's death, and its effect on Henchard's behaviour.

2. What was Henchard's attitude to Farfrae's courtship of Elizabeth-Jane ?

3. What did Henchard do when Newson came back to Caster-bridge a second time ?

4. Describe Henchard's entry into Elizabeth's house at the time of her wedding celebrations.

5. Describe the circumstances of the death of Henchard and state the terms of his will.

6. What strikes you as the most pathetic incident or circumstance of these last chapters ?

7. Put the philosophy of the last paragraph of *The Mayor of Casterbridge* into your own words.

QUESTIONS

GENERAL QUESTIONS

1. Write a short description of the town of Casterbridge.
2. To what extent does Hardy make use of Casterbridge customs or traditions in *The Mayor of Casterbridge* ?
3. Mention any coincidences in the story that seem to you difficult to believe.
4. What do you think was the greatest mistake of Henchard's life ? Give a reasoned answer supporting your choice.
5. To what extent was Henchard himself responsible for the calamities that befell him ?
6. Mention any strange contradictions in Henchard's character.
7. What do we learn of the character of Henchard from the way in which he treats Elizabeth-Jane ?
8. Would you agree that Henchard loves nobody but himself ? Give your reasons.
9. Contrast *either* Farfrae *or* Elizabeth-Jane with Henchard.
10. " He has such a knack of making everything bring him fortune." Illustrate this estimate of Farfrae.
11. At the end of the story would you say that Farfrae is worthy of his wife ? Give your reasons in full.
12. Do you find Elizabeth-Jane too insipid to be interesting ? Justify your decision.
13. Do you admire or pity Elizabeth-Jane ? Give your reasons.
14. Show briefly what part Lucetta plays in the plot of *The Mayor of Casterbridge*.
15. What is the function in the story of the obscure people of Casterbridge ? Write a few comments on them as a group, showing how they contribute to the effect of the novel as a whole, and on Abel Whittle and one other in particular.
16. " Hardy is greatest in his most tragic moments." Do you agree (basing your answer on *The Mayor of Casterbridge*) ?
17. *The Mayor of Casterbridge* has often been called a " pessimistic " book. Say what incidents and characteristics of the novel could have earned it this adjective.
18. Give a short account of two episodes in the story, one revealing humour and the other pathos.
19. Give examples of Hardy's use of (*a*) sympathetic background, (*b*) circumstantial detail, (*c*) contrast. What is the effect of each ?
20. " The good old times ". Comment on this phrase in the light of *The Mayor of Casterbridge*.

CONTEXT QUESTIONS

Answer briefly the questions below each of the following passages.

1. ' You—have—married Mr. Farfrae ! ' cried Elizabeth-Jane, in Nathan tones.
Lucetta bowed. She had recovered herself.

' The bells are ringing on that account,' she said. ' My husband is downstairs. He will live here till a more suitable house is ready for us ; and I have told him that I want you to stay with me just as before.'

' Let me think of it alone,' the girl quickly replied, corking up the turmoil of her feeling with grand control.

(a) What reasons had Lucetta just given to Elizabeth-Jane for marrying Mr. Farfrae ?

(b) What sort of tones are " Nathan tones " ? Explain the allusion.

(c) Why was it natural for Elizabeth to speak " in Nathan tones " on this subject ?

(d) " Let me think of it alone ". There was no need for Elizabeth-Jane to do this. Why not ?

(e) Mention any other occasion when Elizabeth-Jane showed grand self-control.

2.   Passing to and fro the Mayor beheld the unattractive exterior of Farfrae's erection in the West Walk, rick-cloths of different sizes and colours being hung up to the arching trees without any regard to appearance. He was easy in his mind now, for his own preparations far transcended these.

The morning came. The sky, which had been remarkably clear down to within a day or two, was overcast, and the weather threatening, the wind having an unmistakable hint of water in it. Henchard wished he had not been quite so sure about the continuance of a fair season. But it was too late to modify or postpone, and the proceedings went on.

(a) From where had Farfrae obtained the materials for his erection ?

(b) In what ways did Henchard's preparations " far transcend these " ? Where was his entertainment to be held ?

(c) " The morning came ". Which morning ?

(d) On what other occasion did Henchard make a miscalculation about the weather ?

(e) Describe the nature of the " proceedings " at Henchard's entertainment and at Farfrae's.

(f) What mistake (that is, in Henchard's judgment) did Elizabeth-Jane make at Farfrae's entertainment ?

3.   They walked with joined hands, and it could be perceived that this was the act of simple affection. The daughter carried in her outer hand a withy basket of old-fashioned make ; the mother a blue bundle, which contrasted oddly with her black stuff gown.

Reaching the outskirts of the village, they pursued the same track as formerly, and ascended to the fair. Here, too, it was evident that the years had told. Certain mechanical improvements might have been noticed in the roundabouts and highfliers, machines for testing rustic strength and weight, and in the erections devoted to shooting for nuts. But the real business of the fair had considerably dwindled.

(a) " They walked with joined hands ". Why is this worth notice ?
(b) " Ascended to the fair ". Which fair ?
(c) What had caused " the real business of the fair " to dwindle ?
(d) To what particular place in the fair did the mother proceed ? Why ?
(e) What do you understand by a " *withy* basket ", and a " *stuff* gown ? "

4. ' Believe me, Farfrae ; I have come entirely on your own and your wife's account. She is in danger. I know no more ; and they want you to come. Your man has gone the other way in a mistake. O Farfrae ! don't mistrust me —I am a wretched man ; but my heart is true to you still ! '
Farfrae, however, did distrust him utterly.

(a) What had caused Frafrae's wife to be in danger on that particular night ?
(b) " Farfrae, however, did distrust him utterly. " Why ?
(c) What had occasioned Farfrae's change of plan, so that his man had gone the wrong way to find him ?
(d) What in this speech makes you feel that Henchard is out of breath ?

5. ' 'Twas a cannibal deed ! ' deprecated her listeners. ' Gad, then, I won't quite ha'e it,' said Solomon Longways. ' I say it to-day, and 'tis a Sunday morning, and I wouldn't speak wrongfully for a zilver zixpence at such a time. I don't see noo harm in it. To respect the dead is sound doxology ; and I wouldn't sell skellintons—leastwise respectable skellintons—to be varnished for 'natomies, except I were out o' work. But money is scarce, and throats get dry. Why *should* death rob life o' fourpence ? I say there was no treason in it.'

(a) " 'Twas a cannibal deed ! " What deed was this ?
(b) Point out any thing in Solomon Longways' words that show (i) that his religion was only elevated superstition, (ii) that it was a temporising religion, to be put aside when it suited him.
(c) Give an example of a malapropism from the above passage.

What did the speaker really mean ? Give the meaning of the word he uses and of the word he meant.

(d) What is Hardy's purpose in this humorous touch at this point in the story ?

(e) The speech is followed by a very pathetic comment from another of the bystanders. Give its substance and state its purpose in the telling of the story.

(f) Whereabouts were the speakers standing ? How was it that they had time to stand and talk for so long ?

6.   Henchard was disarmed. His old feeling of supercilious pity for womankind in general was intensified by this suppliant appearing here as the double of the first. Moreover, that thoughtless want of foresight which had led to all her trouble remained with poor Lucetta still ; she had come to meet him here in this compromising way without perceiving the risk. Such a woman was very small deer to hunt ; he felt ashamed, lost all zest and desire to humiliate Lucetta there and then, and no longer envied Farfrae his bargain.

(a) In what way did " this suppliant " appear " as the double of the first ? "

(b) What was the immediate cause of this meeting ? Say who arranged it, and for what purpose.

(c) Was the purpose achieved ?

(d) Give another example of Lucetta's " thoughtless want of foresight. "

(e) One of the results of this meeting was the death of Lucetta. How are the two connected ?

7.   Elizabeth-Jane was fond of music ; she could not help pausing to listen ; and the longer she listened the more she was enraptured. She had never heard any singing like this ; and it was evident that the majority of the audience had not heard such frequently, for they were attentive to a much greater degree than usual.

(a) Who was singing ? Where ?

(b) Why was Elizabeth-Jane in that place ?

(c) What type of people were there ?

(d) In what ways did they show their attentiveness to the song ?

(e) What kind of a song was it ?

8.   They sat stiffly side by side at the darkening table, like some Tuscan painting of the two disciples supping at Emmaus. Lucetta, forming the third and haloed figure, was

opposite them ; Elizabeth-Jane, being out of the game, and out of the group, could observe all from afar, like the evangelist who had to write it down ; that there were long spaces of taciturnity, when all exterior circumstance was subdued to the touch of spoons and china, the click of a heel on the pavement under the window, the passing of a wheelbarrow or cart, the whistling of the carter, the gush of water into householders' buckets at the town-pump opposite ; the exchange of greetings among their neighbours, and the rattle of the yokes by which they carried off their evening supply.

' More bread-and-butter ? ' said Lucetta to Henchard and Farfrae equally, holding out between them a plateful of long slices.

(a) Whereabouts was this ?

(b) How did it happen that Henchard and Farfrae were there together ?

(c) " Like some Tuscan painting ". What sort of a painting does this suggest to you ?

(d) " The two disciples supping at Emmaus ". Briefly refer to this Bible incident. Who was " the evangelist who had to write it down " ?

(e) Why does the author draw attention to the noises outside ?

(f) " More bread-and-butter ? " What followed from this homely enquiry ?

9. This reflection, constantly repeated by Henchard to himself, accompanied him everywhere through the day. His mood was no longer that of the rebellious, ironical, reckless misadventurer ; but the leaden gloom of one who has lost all that can make life interesting, or even tolerable. There would remain nobody for him to be proud of, nobody to fortify him ; for Elizabeth-Jane would soon be but as a stranger, and worse. Susan, Farfrae, Lucetta, Elizabeth— all had gone from him, one after one, either by his fault or by his misfortune.

(a) " This reflection ". What reflection ?

(b) Why did Henchard fear that " Elizabeth-Jane would soon be but as a stranger " ?

(c) " And worse ". What is the significance of this ?

(d) Mention another time when a " leaden gloom " settled on Henchard.

(e) " Susan, Frafrae, Lucetta, Elizabeth—all had gone from him, one after one, either by his fault or his misfortune ". Which would you say it was, in each case, by his fault or by his misfortune ?

10. ' I came here for the sake of Elizabeth ; for myself, if you tell me to leave again to-morrow morning, and never come near you more, I am content to go.'

' Now, now ; we don't want to hear that,' said Henchard gently. ' Of course you won't leave again. Think over the plan I have proposed for a few hours ; and if you can't hit upon a better one we'll adopt it. I have to be away for a day or two on business, unfortunately ; but during that time you can get lodgings—the only ones in the town fit for you are those over the china-shop in High Street—and you can also look for a cottage.'

(a) Where was this conversation held ?
(b) Why was this place chosen ? By whom ?
(c) Was it an appropriate place ?
(d) " I came here for the sake of Elizabeth ? What in the story proves this to be true ?
(e) " The plan I have proposed ". What was the plan ?
(f) " Over the china-shop in High Street ". Why does Hardy put this detailed information into Henchard's speech ?

Key to Context Questions

(1) XXX, 247, (2) XVI, 119, (3) III, 21, (4) XL, 327, (5) XVIII, 137–138, (6) XXXV, 287, (7) VIII, 58, (8) XXVI, 207, (9) XLI, 338–339, (10) XI, 84–85.